To our parents, Lorna Lee and Ian and Mary Uhlmann.

Contents

Dancing
the Psalms

More often than not, if one hears of a sacred dance taking place, it has been done to a hymn: words and music. Sacred dance can be more than just that. It is about time that we began to explore other possibilities for sacred dance. We will now look at a psalm and see how simple dance movements can enhance and bring to life the emotions, the pleas, and the frustrations that the psalmist sang about.

There are many ways of going about this. One way is for the psalm to be read by the lector. When the congregation says the response, a dancer can lead them in simple gestures that have been choreographed to the words of the response. For example, the response to the psalm "I Lift Up My Soul" (St. Louis Jesuits) is, "To you Yahweh, I lift up my soul O my God." While being led by the dancer, the congregation takes their right hands and brings them up slowly in front of their bodies, raising them high and reaching out in front of them with their palms facing upward.

Another possibility is for a dancer or dancers to interpret the psalm through bodily movements. If the movement takes place at the same time as the psalm is read, it is important that the dancers and the lector rehearse together so that the lector reads at a pace that suits the dancers while observing the necessary pauses. Remember, the lector reads to accompany the dancers and not the reverse.

A third possibility is that the dancer(s) may wish to learn the psalm and recite it as they interpret it. This takes a great deal of skill and is not always easy to do.

The following is a simple movement interpretation to Psalm 8:

PSALM 8: Yahweh, our Lord

(DANCER faces the congregation. Slides the right foot forward and, placing all the weight on the front leg, bends the knee slightly. Head tilts back slightly and the arms extend forward with the palms facing upward.)

PSALM 8: How great Your Name throughout all the earth.

(DANCER moves the left foot out to the side in a deep wide position. Both knees are bent. The arms swing up over the head, cross in front of the body, and now extend shoulder height sideways with the palms extended upward.)

PSALM 8: Above the heavens is your majesty chanted.

(DANCER keeping feet in the same position, the dancer takes both arms and extends them straight overhead with palms facing each other.)

PSALM 8: By the mouths of children

(DANCER straightens knees. Slides the left foot across the body and places it diagonally right with the foot placed firmly on the ground. Bends the left leg and gradually kneels on the right knee. Extends the right arm upward, focusing the eyes

toward the right hand. Body leans slightly backward. Places the left hand delicately against the left cheek with the palm facing outward.)

PSALM 8: Babes in arms

(DANCER stands and leans, weight onto the front left leg. Bends the knee. Stretches the right leg out behind and points the toe. With the right arm still extended upward, extends the left arm out diagonally to the left corner. Body and head are turned slightly to the left diagonal.)

PSALM 8: You set your stronghold firm against your foes to subdue your enemies.

(DANCER brings both feet into an open wide position. Knees straighten and dancer faces the front. The weight transfers to the left side so that the left knee bends. Dancer takes the left arm up overhead with a clenched fist. The right hand grasps the left wrist.)

PSALM 8: I look at the heavens made by your fingers

(DANCER runs around in a wide circle with arms slightly behind the body. Head tilts back.)

PSALM 8: At the moon and the stars you set in place.

(DANCER continues run. The run is done only once.)

PSALM 8: Ah, what is man that you should spare a thought for him?

(DANCER stops suddenly and faces the congregation. Feet are apart, head erect, and arms firmly stretched down to the side. The feet are apart in a wide, comfortable position.)

PSALM 8: The son of man that you should care for him

(*DANCER takes two turning movements to the left to finish in the same position.*)

PSALM 8: You have made him less than a God

(*DANCER brings both feet together and rises on them. At the same time, s/he takes both arms and swings them (going to the right) up above the body, bringing them down by the left and taking them out to stretch shoulder height to the right.*)

PSALM 8: You have crowned him with glory and splendour

(*DANCER lunges onto the left foot out into a diagonally left direction. Arms extend comfortably backward. Palms face downward.*)

PSALM 8: Made him lord over the work of your hands.

(*DANCER brings both legs and feet together to stand in an upright position facing the congregation. Extends arms diagonally forward, bending them slightly at the elbows. Palms face upward.*)

PSALM 8: Set all things under his feet.

(*DANCER, keeping the same position, brings both hands back, diagonally stretching down to the ground.*)

This is only one idea of what can be done with psalms and with readings. As mentioned before, it is most important that the reader and the dancer(s) rehearse. Timing is crucial. The pauses between each thought and movement have to be carefully planned so that the psalm will flow without loosing its meaning.

The following is a simple movement interpretation to Psalm 100:

PSALM 100: Acclaim Yahweh all the earth

(The DANCERS, a group of 7 or 8 people, are bowed over on their knees and scattered at different points. They suddenly reach out in all directions, some going up, some going down, and others reaching outward.)

PSALM 100: Serve Yahweh gladly

(DANCERS stand and lunge to their right. They bring their hands from top right in an arc downward across their bodies and up again to top left.)

PSALM 100: Come into his presence with songs of joy

(DANCERS take four running steps into a centre point. With each step they clap once: once at knee height, once at waist height, once at shoulder height, and once high above their heads. They then freeze.)

PSALM 100: Know that Yahweh is God

(DANCERS spin out from the centre point two turns moving to the right, arms in front and palms facing upward. Freeze.)

PSALM 100: He made us, we belong to Him.

(DANCERS kneel on one leg and run hands downward from head to floor and out to side with palms facing the ground. Freeze.)

PSALM 100: We are His people, the flock that He shepherds.

(DANCERS stand, turn to the right, and run into the centre point. Stand in a circle, interlock arms over each other's shoulders. All heads bow forward into the circle. Everyone bends slightly at the knees.)

PSALM 100: Walk through His porticos giving thanks. Enter His courts praising Him.

(DANCERS straighten knees and stand up straight. Leave arms on each other's shoulders. All walk together four steps to the right, commencing with the right leg. Then release arms quickly and clap hands once above the head as they turn outward from the circle by their right. Facing out of the circle, bring hands out to the front, waist high, with palms facing upward.)

PSALM 100: Give thanks to Him, bless His name

(DANCERS bring both feet together and, as they bend their knees, bring both arms down and across their bodies and raise them up high above the head. The head tilts slightly back.)

PSALM 100: Yahweh is good, His love is everlasting

(DANCERS turn once again into the centre of the circle by the left and bring both hands into the centre of the circle with the palms facing upward. All fingertips should be touching.)

PSALM 100: His faithfulness endures from age to age.

(DANCERS leaving the left hand in the centre of the circle, turn to the right and lunge out of the circle on the right leg. At the same time, bring the right hand out from the circle and down, placing it at waist height, palm upward and reaching out.)

The Prodigal Son

The story of the prodigal son is a drama designed for a narrator and chorus. The number of people in the chorus is unimportant—in fact, the more the better—but I would advise that you use no less than six players. Timing is extremely important. The chorus must be in unison and their response must be uniform. Various gestures and special effects (such as streamers, kazoos, and banners) may be used by the chorus to make the presentation more visually exciting.

NARRATOR: There was a man who had two sons.

CHORUS: One (*one person stands*), Two (*another person stands*).

NARRATOR: The younger son said,

SON 1: Hey daddy, could I have half the property, which belongs to me?

NARRATOR: So the father divided the property, and a few days later the younger son took all his money and drove off.

CHORUS: BRRRRRM. Byeeeeeee.

NARRATOR: But he squandered his money in a life of debauchery.

CHORUS: (*shocked*) OOOOOOOOOOOOOH !

NARRATOR: When he had spent it all he was left penniless.

CHORUS: Tough luck.

NARRATOR: So he was hired by a local to feed the pigs.

CHORUS: OINK OINK. Er Yuck.

NARRATOR: He got so hungry...

CHORUS: (*holding tummies*) OOOOH.

NARRATOR: ...that he would have even eaten the pigs' food.

CHORUS: (*hands to mouth*) UGH.

NARRATOR: Then he came to his senses.

CHORUS: Thank goodness.

NARRATOR: And he said,

CHORUS: (*expectantly*) What did he say?

NARRATOR: (*to the chorus*) Hang on. (*To the audience*) And he said,

SON 1: I think I'll go home and say to the old man, "I'm sorry, dad."

CHORUS: (*to the son*) About time.

NARRATOR: So he headed off home—on foot.

CHORUS: Left, right, left, right.

NARRATOR: While he was still a long way off, his father saw him.

CHORUS: LOOK! (*pointing to audience*) It's Sabastian. OOOOH.

SON 1: Daddy, I'm sorry.

CHORUS: AAAH (*applaud*).

NARRATOR: And his father, who was a real good bloke, took him back.

CHORUS: Hurray!!

NARRATOR: And they started to have a party.

CHORUS: (*to the tune of "Happy Birthday"*) Oh Sabastian is back, yes Sabastian is back, and we are so happy, 'cause Sabastian is back.

A VOICE: What about the older brother?

CHORUS: Who?

NARRATOR: Yes, he was really annoyed, because he hadn't even been invited to the party and he said,

SON 2: Listen daddy-o: How come you gave this creep, who wasted all your money, a party?

CHORUS: Yeah! How come?

NARRATOR: And the father said,

FATHER: Well, it's like this: Everything that I have now belongs to you, but we should be happy because your brother, who was lost, is found.

CHORUS: HURRAY!! (*sing chorus again*) Oh Sabastian is back...

NARRATOR: Now, if this is the way an ordinary bloke treats his son,

CHORUS: (*expectantly*) Yeah?

NARRATOR: ...how much better will our Father in heaven treat us?

CHORUS: (*all look at each other and nod*)

Royal Waiters

(The stage is bare except for four or five chairs in a line across the front of the stage. They form a barrier. Four players enter and take up their positions behind the chairs. They take out streamers and whistles, clickers and flags and begin to cheer and wave frantically. They are obviously very excited.)

CHARACTER A: Hurray! Let's hear it for the King.

CHARACTER B: Long live the King!

CHARACTER C: Royalty forever!

CHARACTER D: Good on yer, your majesty!

(They keep up their fuss for some time, then one by one they begin to tire of their cheering. They look at their watches and the noise gradually dies down. The flags go limp. They look bored.)

A: Bit late ain't he?

B: Yeah.

C: Mind you, it doesn't surprise me—just another example of your ruling class's flagrant disregard for the working people.

D: Now, now. He does have a long way to come.

B: Is that so? Where is he from?

D: Heaven.

OTHERS: Heaven!

D: Oh yes. I thought you knew, he's not just any King, He's the King of Kings—God's Son. He's been keeping people waiting for ages.

A: A bit rude, isn't he?

D: Oh no, my friend. Eye has not seen nor ear heard the greatness of the mind of God.

A: Still think he's rude.

B: Yeah.

C: Yeah.

D: Look, you carry on as if you're the only people he's ever kept waiting.

C: You mean he does this regularly?

D: Oh constantly! He kept Abraham waiting for a son until he was ninety-nine.

OTHERS: NINETY-NINE!

B: He's lucky he could still walk let alone have children. Mind you, I wish I'd have waited before I had my Denny. Now there's a horror of a child.

D: Not only that, he made Moses and the people of Israel wander for forty years in the desert before they found the promised land.

C: WHAT! Forty years! I didn't even bring a cut lunch.

D: You see, God has kept everyone waiting. But he always comes good on His promises, and they are really worth waiting for. People have been waiting for His Son for centuries.

A: Well, what's the point?

D: Eh?

A: What's the point of all these generations of people looking wistfully skyward, waiting for this God to send His Son?

D: Well, when He comes He will bring peace on earth and harmony, and the lion will lie down with the lamb and all that.

B: But what's He going to do about inflation? I mean lions lying down with sheep is all very well, but how about the important things in life, eh?

D: But when the King comes, none of those things will matter any more, you'll see.

C: What's He look like then?

D: What do you mean, what does He look like?

C: It's quite obvious, I thought. How will we know when He comes if we don't know what He looks like?

D: How should I know what He looks like! But when He comes we'll just know it's Him, you'll see.

C: Well that's that then; I'm off. I haven't got time to waste on some celestial fairy tale.

D: Look, hang on, just wait a little longer. It will be worth it when He comes.

A: Look mate, if past form is any indication, we will all be dead by the time He comes.

B: Yeah, let's face it. God may have eons to sit around waiting, but He's immortal; me, I've got better things to do. Come on, let's go.

D: Wait, please wait, just a little longer.

A: No mate, sorry.

B: Bye.

C: See you later.

(*D is left alone. He looks around at the streamers and looks exasperated. Then he notices the audience.*)

D: Well, what are you all waiting for? (*He walks off.*)

Max's Christmas

"Max's Christmas" is a monologue. Its interpretation is very much up to the individual performer, so there are no detailed instructions on how this should be staged. Max (or Maxine) is a simple character, and his reflections on Christmas are simple, so the staging should reflect this. I imagine a bare stage (sanctuary) dimly lit except for one highlighted area. Max may be sweeping, and when he comes into the lighted area he stops and begins his prayer; when he is finished he simply begins sweeping again and moves off.

MAX: God, hey God, remember me? The name's Max. Uh, look, I'm really sorry to be bothering you like this; I mean, especially today. Look, I know it's your Son's birthday and I'm real sorry to be calling you now. You've probably got a party going on up there with Jesus and Mary and the angels and that, and the last thing that you want is some nobody ringing you up and pestering you with his problems. I can just see it: you all standing around singing "Happy Birthday," Jesus just set to blow out 2000-odd candles when all of a sudden the phone rings. Wouldn't you know it!

"Who's that, Mary?"

"Oh, just that pest Max with his problems again."

Yeah, that's me. So look, I'll try to be real quick so that you can get back in time for your coffee and ice cream.

Actually it's because it's Christmas that I'm ringing; that's the problem, see. Don't get me wrong: it's not actually Christmas that's the problem; I really think that that's one of your best ideas.

You see, I just came from the church. Well I always like to go at Christmas, especially Midnight Mass when they sing all those lovely songs and carols and stuff. It was really nice.

Well, it was while we were singing that song. You know the one. I've told you about it before. How's it go again? Da, da, da—yeah, that's it:

"Joy to the World the Lord has come"

"Let the earth receive her King."

That's when it hit me, POW just like that. I looked around at the people in the church; they seemed happy but I got wondering. I wondered how far our joy was really going: was it going to the whole world—you know, the WHOLE WORLD, not just the church where I was. Just then the church seemed so small, just like our joy—so small. A little bit of joy in a little box, not joy for the WHOLE WORLD. I know; I've seen the world and at the moment it isn't a happy place.

I see things: wars, murders, hunger and bombs—bombs that can blow up everything. How about that then? We may not be able to fill the whole world with joy, but we can blow the whole place up if we want to. It really frightens me sometimes. So many people hating, so many people hurting, so little joy of any kind.

Well then I got angry. You know I've got a temper. I've talked about it before. It was just that I didn't know who to get angry at: the people in the Church, the government, me, or just anyone. I hate to say it, especially today, but I even got a little angry at you, God. I thought, well, I thought if you loved us all so much, how come you let this thing happen? Why didn't Jesus fix it all up when He came; why do people have to hurt so much?

Then after I thought some more, I kinda had a change of heart. I guess Jesus did tell us all we needed to know; we just aren't good listeners.

I like to build things, you see, and I thought, well, I guess Jesus gave us the material to build all the joy we wanted, but we just built other stuff, like bombs and things like that.

I thought—and I hope you don't take any offence to this, God—but I thought it's all well and good to go to church at Christmas and sing about joy, but if we don't get up off our pews and go out of the church and spread some of it around, we might as well be singing "Twinkle Twinkle Little Star."

So, thanks for listening, God. I really learned a lot this Christmas. I'd better let you get back to the party now. Say hello to everyone for me.

Give Jesus my best.

See ya soon, God.

Simon the Magician

CAST:
Announcer
Simon the Magician
Crowd (approximately 7 people)
Peter the Apostle

PROPS:
A cardboard megaphone
A billboard with the words SIMON THE MAGICIAN
Plastic flowers
A sheet of plain paper
A top hat
A stuffed toy rabbit that fits inside the hat

The announcer walks onto the stage and places the billboard, which says SIMON THE MAGICIAN, in a prominent position. The crowd at this point is just walking about aimlessly.)

ANNOUNCER: Roll up, roll up. See the magnificent Simon perform wonders that will astound you. See Simon levitate before your very eyes; see him produce bunnies from his hat

19

where previously there were no bunnies. Simon the Magician, a truly momentous man of our time. It is reputed his power comes from the high god himself. Let's hear it for Simon. He is the divine power that is called great.

(*Simon appears from the side of the stage and bows slightly to the audience. The crowd rushes across and stands directly behind Simon.*)

CROWD: Hurray Simon, hurray. He is the divine power that is called great.

(*Simon gestures to the audience that there is nothing up his sleeves, then he whips out a bunch of flowers from one of his sleeves. The crowd is astonished.*)

CROWD: OHHH. Hurray Simon, hurray. He is the divine power that is called great.

(*Simon is obviously pleased with his success. He takes a piece of ordinary paper, shows both sides to the crowd, then begins to frantically fold the sheet of paper. Everyone looks on expectantly. Simon produces a paper jet plane and throws it across the stage. The crowd goes berserk.*)

CROWD: Hurray Simon, hurray. He is the divine power that is called great.

SIMON: Thank you, thank you.

(*The crowd continues to cheer Simon until everyone, Simon included, notices that another figure has entered the scene from the other side of the stage. This person is slow-handclapping Simon. The noise subsides and everyone stares at the new arrival.*)

SIMON: Who are you, stranger?

PETER: My name is Peter.

SIMON: And weren't you impressed with my feats of magic?

PETER: Well, don't get me wrong: you were good, quite good, but to be honest those sort of tricks don't really grab me. Let's face it, what cosmic significance is there in pulling flowers out of the air? Besides, I know a better sort of power than yours. Someone who makes you look like the tooth fairy.

SIMON: Who is this person you speak of?

PETER: His name is Jesus.

(The crowd rushes over from their position behind Simon and stands directly behind Peter.)

CROWD: Hurray Jesus, hurray. He is the divine power that is called great.

(Simon takes the hat from his head and says,)

SIMON: Can your Jesus do this?

(Simon pulls a stuffed rabbit from his hat. The crowd is astonished and they all run back and stand behind Simon.)

CROWD: Hurray Simon, hurray. He is the divine power that is called great.

PETER: Impressive, very impressive, Simon, but I was with Jesus when He walked on water and when He raised a man from the dead. But, far more important, He gave people a reason for living.

(The crowd runs over and stands behind Peter.)

CROWD: Hurray Jesus, hurray. He is the divine power that is called great.

SIMON: Well, where is this Jesus?

PETER: Oh, He died!

(The crowd look at each other.)

CROWD: DIED!

(They all wander over and stand behind Simon. This time they are less enthusiastic as they cheer.)

CROWD: Hurray Simon, Hurray. He is the divine power that is called great.

SIMON: Well. I guess that's the end of that. Pity, really, that competition is what this business is all about.

PETER: Well, that's not the end actually. You see, the power in Jesus was so great that he rose from the dead.

(This time the crowd can hardly contain themselves and they all rush over behind Peter.)

CROWD: Hurray Jesus, hurray. He is the divine power that is called great.

SIMON: But, but, I can levitate. Look.

(Simon starts to take small, pathetic, hops into the air, flapping his arms frantically. The crowd looks confused. They look at one another, shrug their shoulders, and begin very slowly

to walk towards Simon. When they are halfway across the stage, Peter calls,)

PETER: But is this really what is important to you?

(The crowd stops, turns, and looks at Peter.)

SIMON: Of course it's important, you fool. I can fly. I can fly. (*He continues to hop into the air.*)

(The crowd turns and looks at Simon.)

PETER: But Jesus can give you new life.

(The crowd turns and looks at Peter.

SIMON: But I will give you wings. (*He continues hopping.*)

PETER: Believe in Jesus. He is the ONLY power that is real.

(*Half the crowd looks at Peter.*)

SIMON: NO, believe in me.

(The other half of the crowd looks at Simon.)

ANNOUNCER: (*looking at the audience*) Well, you decide: Who will you follow?

Noah

This drama is designed for the five- to seven-year-old age group. Some children will be the ARK, some will be ANIMALS, and one will be NOAH. Before reading the narrative, you will need to organize the ark depending on the number of children in your class. Use your imagination, but the formation could look like the following:

The animal group will need to be in pairs and decide upon the kind of animal they will be and the noises and movements they will make. Go through the story a couple of times with them. The working area (stage, classroom, whatever) starts with Noah and the children who will be the ark on one side and the children who are the animals on the other. For example,

Ark and Noah   Animals

Front

NARRATOR: Once upon a time, long long ago, the world became a very bad place, and there were lots of nasty people in
it. So God decided to make it rain. It would rain so hard and
so long that all the world would be covered up with water.

In all the world, there was only one person who was God's
friend. His name was Noah. (*Noah walks forward from the
side and stands facing the front.*) So God told Noah to build
a boat. But not just any ordinary boat. It would be called an
ark, and it would be a very, very big boat.

So Noah began to build the ark. (*Noah begins to build the
ark with the other children.*)

It took a long time.

And the people laughed at Noah because he was building a
boat so far from the water. (*All the children who have not so
far been used in the ark and all the children who are not building or are animals begin to laugh and then stop.*)

Then God told Noah the reason why the boat had to be so
big. Noah had to get two of every animal in the world, one boy
and one girl animal, and put them into the boat.

There were... (*At this point the animals begin to come in
and the narrator reads out the animals name as they come
in.*)

When Noah had filled up the boat with animals, he got in with his family and shut the door.

Then it began to rain and rain. (*The animals will make the rain sound by tapping their thighs with their hands.*)

It rained very hard. (*Rain noise gets louder.*)

And the animals got frightened. (*Animals all make their noises.*)

Even Noah got frightened. (*Noah looking suitably scared.*)

And soon the boat was afloat on a giant sea.

The boat rocked backward and forward and backward and forward. (*The children who are the ark rock from side to side.*)

It rained for forty days and forty nights. (*Rain noise and rocking continues.*)

Then it stopped. (*Rain stops, but the boat keeps rocking gently.*)

And after a long time, the water went down and the ark came to rest on a mountain. (*Rocking stops.*)

So Noah came out of the ark. (*Noah comes out.*)

He waved goodbye to all the animals.

He waved goodbye to the... (*name the animals as they come out.*)

And God made the rainbow to show that he loved Noah and all the animals and that He would never flood the world again.

(End)

The story has been broken down to its main parts for simplicity's sake, and various details such as the dove at the end of the story have been left out. Use your imaginations to adapt the story in whatever way suits your needs best. Not everything you do has to be presented. This drama might work best as simply a teaching tool.

Parable of the Two Sons

(This parable comes from Matthew 22:28-32.)

The players all stand in a line, mid-stage centre, facing the front. The narrator can stand anywhere as long as s/he is not in the way. The principal characters will all come from the line (i.e., father and two children). The purpose of the other members of the group, who are not principal characters, is to respond to the story, add colour, humour, insight, and generally make the whole picture more interesting. You can suit yourself as to how many people you use in the group, but any more than eight will be too cluttered.

NARRATOR: There once was a man who had two sons.

(*Father steps forward and smiles. The group politely applauds.*)

NARRATOR: He was very wealthy and owned a chain of successful hamburger restaurants.

(*Father smiles.*)

29

NARRATOR: Now one day he received an urgent phone call from one of his nearby restaurants.

GROUP: Ring ring, ring ring. Hello.

(*Father mimes picking up the phone.*)

NARRATOR: They were short-staffed and urgently needed someone to come and help out for the afternoon.

(*Group and father place one hand over their mouths with a "what shall we do?" look on their faces.*)

NARRATOR: Then the father had an idea.

GROUP: Ding! (*Their faces light up as they all raise their right index finger.*)

NARRATOR: He decided to send his oldest son, Zack.

(*Father clicks fingers and Zack steps forward from the group.*)

NARRATOR: Now Zack was a bit of a worry for his father. He was not what you'd call a star student.

GROUP: Ohhhh.

(*All concerned.*)

NARRATOR: No, he spent all his time listening to the latest rock music.

GROUP: (*becomes impressed*) Hey.

(*Zack smiles and nods knowingly.*)

NARRATOR: Watching MTV.

GROUP: (*warming to Zack*) Yeah!

(Zack shrugs his shoulders.)

NARRATOR: Doing Michael Jackson impersonations.

GROUP: (*getting really excited*) Woah!

(*Zack assumes a rock star pose and freezes momentarily.*)

NARRATOR: And rap dancing.

(*Zack assumes a rap dance pose.*)

(*This is the final straw, and the group jumps up and down, claps their hands, and generally makes a great deal of noise until the narrator turns and fixes them with a steely glare. At this point the group realizes that they have lost their decorum and move back into their places a little embarrassed.*)

NARRATOR: Now when his father asked him about working in the shop he was less than amused.

(*Group and father all point to the left and freeze. They stay frozen.*)

ZACK: What! Aw, listen Dad, I've got much better things to do than that. I wanna buy a new record, and I'm going to a party tonight. I'd love to help but you know how it is.

(*During Zack's speech the group and the father stay frozen, but their faces fall and become sad. Zack walks off to the right a few steps, then turns and comes back to his father, still frozen, and says,*)

ZACK: By the way, could you lend me $10.00?

(*His father, with his left arm still frozen, reaches into his right-hand pocket and gives Zack the money. Then he returns to his frozen position, pointing left, face still fallen, as Zack goes off to the right a few steps and stops, facing the audience.*)

NARRATOR: So off Zack went, to his father's disappointment, but he hadn't gone far when he had second thoughts. He really did love his father. So Zack changed his mind and went to work at the hamburger restaurant.

(*Zack looks at the money his father gave him, puts it in his pocket, and walks back to the left between the father and the group. The father stays frozen, but the group, who sees Zack, begin trying to get the father's attention. One comes forward and begins to wave his/her arms frantically and points to Zack, who is now frozen front-left of stage. The group member tries again to get the father's attention, but to no avail. The father remains frozen still pointing left. The group member becomes exhausted and gives up. S/he returns to the group.*)

NARRATOR: Meanwhile the father decided to call his second child: his daughter, Prudence.

(*Father breaks from freeze, clicks his fingers, and motions for Prudence to come forward. Up until this time Prudence has been a member of the group. She steps forward from the line to stand beside her father.*)

NARRATOR: Now Prudence was an excellent student.

GROUP: (*slightly interested*) Ohhhhh!

NARRATOR: She always did her homework.

GROUP: (*amazed*) What!

NARRATOR: She didn't care for rock music.

GROUP: (*stunned*) Huh!

NARRATOR: And she always crawled to the teachers.

GROUP: Er, Yuck.

NARRATOR: Prudence was so sweet, it was sickening.

GROUP: (*holding tummies*) Blahh!

NARRATOR: Her father asked her to go and work for him in the restaurant.

PRUDENCE: Oh daddy, I'd really love to go.

(*Father and group still frozen but with big smiles as they nod their heads.*)

NARRATOR: And she skipped off.

(*Prudence skips off to the left a few paces and then freezes.*)

NARRATOR: But she hadn't gone far when she had second thoughts. She really didn't like hamburgers; she preferred health food. And she just knew frying chips all day would ruin her hands. So she changed her mind and went off to the library to do some extra studying.

(*Prudence skips in between the group and her father. Father stays frozen as group once again try to gain his attention. A different member comes forward and tries frantically to make him see what has happened, but to no avail. S/he returns to the main group.*)

(*Father breaks from his position and moves to centre of stage. He looks to the right and to the left; as he does this, he holds out his right hand and then his left as the narrator reads.*)

NARRATOR: Now which of these two children do you think did his father's will?

GROUP: (*half look at Zack; half look at Prudence.*)

Emmaus

CAST:
Narrator
Jesus
Two disciples

You will also need the song "Are Not Our Hearts" from *Hi God* by Carey Landry.

This short play and dance would be suitable for a senior primary or junior secondary class.

NARRATOR: Two of the disciples were on their way to a village called Emmaus, seven miles from Jerusalem, and they were talking together about all that had happened. Now as they talked this over, Jesus himself came up and walked by their side; but something prevented them from recognizing him.

JESUS: What matters are you discussing as you walk along?

NARRATOR: They stopped short, their faces downcast.

ALL: Are not our hearts... (*sing one verse only.*)

NARRATOR: Then one answered him.

DISCIPLE 1: You must be the only person in Jerusalem who does not know the things that have been happening there these last few days.

JESUS: What things?

DISCIPLE 2: All about Jesus of Nazareth, who proved he was a great prophet by the things that he said and did in the sight of God and the whole people; and how the chief priests and leaders handed him over to be sentenced to death and crucified.

DISCIPLE 1: Two whole days have gone by since it happened; and some women from our group have astounded us; they went to the tomb in the early morning, and when they did not find the body, they came back to us. They had seen a vision of angels who declared he was alive.

ALL: Are not our hearts... (*sing one verse only.*)

DISCIPLE 2: Some of our friends went to the tomb and found everything exactly as the women reported, but of Him they saw nothing.

JESUS: You foolish men! So slow to believe the full message of the prophets: was it not ordained that Christ should suffer and so enter into this glory?

NARRATOR: When they drew near the village to which they were going, he made as if to go on; but they pressed Him to stay with them.

DISCIPLE 1: It is nearly evening and the day is almost over.

NARRATOR: So he went in to stay with them.

ALL: Are not our hearts... (*sing one verse only.*)

NARRATOR: Now, while he was with them at table, he took the bread and said the blessing; then he broke it and handed it to them. And their eyes were opened and they recognized him, but he had vanished from their sight. Then they said to each other,

DISCIPLE 2: Didn't our hearts burn within us as he talked on the road and explained the scriptures to us?

ALL: Are not our hearts... (*sing one verse only, then sing both verses while dancers perform the following. This dance can be done in a circle with any number of people.*)

(*While VERSE 1 is sung, the DANCERS, facing anti-clockwise, walk around in the circle, commencing on their right foot. At the same time they bring their hands into the centre of their chests and raise them up high above their heads. This is done four times.*

For VERSE 2, the DANCERS, facing the centre of the circle, take hold of hands and walk four steps into the centre of the circle. At the same time, they raise their hands up high. They then take four steps backward to their original places and bring their hands down. This is repeated once more.)

Advent Play with Dance

This is a movement/drama for upper primary and junior secondary students, taken from the Gospel of Luke.

SCENE ONE

NARRATOR: This is the Gospel according to Luke.

The angel Gabriel was sent by God as a messenger to a small town of Galilee that was called Nazareth. In this town the angel would find a young girl who was engaged to a man called Joseph. Her name was Mary. The angel found Mary in her home and said to her,

GABRIEL: Rejoice Mary! The Lord is with you.

MARY: What do you mean?

GABRIEL: Mary, do not be frightened. God is happy with you. You have been chosen from all other women to bear a son, and you must name him Jesus. He will be great and will be called the Son of the Most High. He will receive the throne of his ancestor David.

MARY: How can this happen? I don't understand.

GABRIEL: God's Holy Spirit will come upon you. Your child will be Holy and will be called the Son of God. Nothing is impossible.

MARY: Let all that you have said happen.

SCENE TWO

NARRATOR: Mary set out on a long journey to visit her cousin Elizabeth, who was also expecting a baby. On reaching Elizabeth's house, Mary went in.

ELIZABETH: Of all the women, Mary, you are the most blessed, and blessed also is the baby within your womb. Why am I honoured by a visit from the mother of my Lord? Mary, you are blessed because you believed that the promise made to you by God would be fulfilled.

(Here I would suggest one of two ideas. The Magnificat can either be spoken as well as dramatized through bodily movement by Mary, or it can be spoken by the narrator while Mary interprets it through movement.)

MARY OR NARRATOR: My soul proclaims the greatness of the Lord and my spirit exults in God my Saviour.

(MOVEMENT: Face the front with feet together and bring both arms out sideward until shoulder high. Slowly step backward on the right foot and bring both arms down to the side and bend slightly over the front foot. Toe should be pointed.)

MARY OR NARRATOR: Because he has looked upon his lowly handmaid.

(*MOVEMENT: Move back to the original starting position with feet together and arms at shoulder height extended toward the side.*)

MARY OR NARRATOR: Yes, from this day onward all generations shall call me blessed.

(*MOVEMENT: Take both arms to the left side with the right hand on top of the left and bring both arms slowly forward across the body to extend to the right side.*)

MARY OR NARRATOR: For the Almighty has done great things for me and Holy is His name.

(*MOVEMENT: Bring both arms up overhead with hands together and palms facing outward as if framing God's name with the hands.*)

MARY: And His mercy reaches from age to age for those who fear Him.

(*MOVEMENT: Bring arms down to extend outward with palms facing upward. Then take right arm to the right side and left arm to the left side.*)

MARY OR NARRATOR: He has shown the power of His arm.

(*MOVEMENT: Raise right arm into the air with fist closed and bring left arm down to the side.*)

MARY OR NARRATOR: He has routed the proud of heart.

(*MOVEMENT: Kneel on left knee and bring both hands into the centre of the chest. Bow head slightly.*)

MARY OR NARRATOR: He has pulled down princes from their thrones,

(*MOVEMENT: Stay in the above position.*)

MARY OR NARRATOR: and exalted the lowly.

(*MOVEMENT: Raise head and stand with both feet apart and the arms raised in an open "V" position.*)

MARY OR NARRATOR: The hungry He has filled with good things,

(*MOVEMENT: Step to the right on the right foot and lunge to the right pointing the left toe. At the same time, bring both arms to stretch out forward with palms facing upward.*)

MARY OR NARRATOR: the rich sent empty away.

(*MOVEMENT: Stepping back onto both feet, take left arm out to the side with palm facing upward. Head is turned to face the right side.*)

MARY OR NARRATOR: He has come to the help of Israel His servant, mindful of His mercy.

(*MOVEMENT: Step forward and extend both arms forward with palms facing upward.*)

MARY OR NARRATOR: According to the promise He made to our ancestors

(*MOVEMENT: Step backward, keeping arms in the same position.*)

MARY OR NARRATOR: of His mercy to Abraham and his descendants for ever.

MOVEMENT: (*Kneel on both knees with arms reaching upward in a "V" position. Sit back slightly on knees.*)

Sower and
the Seed (1)

This is a narrative, which means that the action is taking place as the story is being read. The characters in the mime are:

The Narrator
The Sower
The Seeds (4 groups of 3 people)
The Thorns (1 group of 3 people)

The setting should look like this:

A

BBB   CCC   EEE   FFF
                 DDD

G

A: The Sower
B,C,D,F: The Seeds
E: The Thorns
G: The Narrator

All the characters are standing with their backs to the audience. We are now ready to begin.

NARRATOR: Imagine a sower going out to sow.

(ACTION: SOWER turns around very slowly to face the front. He picks up his basket, which is on the ground at his left side and throws some seed in the direction of group B.

GROUP B turns around slowly to face the front. They then kneel on both knees, heads and body bowed over low to the ground.

SOWER repeats his action of throwing the seeds in the direction of group C.

GROUP C turns around slowly to face the front. They kneel on both knees, heads and body bowed over low to the ground.

SOWER then repeats the action of throwing the seeds, this time in the direction of group D.

GROUP D repeats the turning and kneeling action that was done by the previous groups.

When group D turns so does group E. They also bow over in the kneeling position at the same time as group D moves.

SOWER again repeats the throwing actions, this time toward group F.

GROUP F turns and likewise kneels to take on the bowing position.)

NARRATOR: As he sowed, some seeds fell on the edge of the path, and the birds of the air came and ate them up.

(ACTION: GROUP B comes up very slowly into a tall kneeling position. Their arms are at shoulder height and bent at the elbows.

With sudden and sharp movements starting with the right hand, they begin to block out the birds coming to get them. Four swift blocks are used: right, left, right, left.

GROUP B then falls back into their kneeling position.).

NARRATOR: Others fell on patches of rock where they found little soil and sprang up right away because there was no depth of earth.

(ACTION: GROUP C comes up in the same way that Group B did.)

NARRATOR: But as soon as the sun came up, they were scorched and, not having any roots, they withered away.

(ACTION: Very slowly the seeds become limp and lifeless and begin to sink back into the ground. They return to their original position.)

NARRATOR: Others fell among thorns.

(ACTION: GROUP D comes up very slowly to a kneeling position the same as Group B, but this time they rest on the backs of their heels.)

NARRATOR: And the thorns grew up and choked them.

(ACTION: GROUP E comes up in the same manner. They come up into a tall kneeling position. They look at each other and then place their hands around the necks of group D who begin to "choke" [very slowly]. Both GROUPS D and E return to their original position.)

NARRATOR: Others fell on rich soil and produced their crop, some one hundredfold.

(ACTION: The first seed in GROUP F stands up on both feet. Arms are once again bent at shoulder height.)

NARRATOR: Some sixty.

(ACTION: The second seed in GROUP F rises to a full kneeling position. Arms are the same as with the first seed.)

NARRATOR: Some thirty.

(ACTION: The third seed in GROUP F rises to a kneeling position but sitting back on heels. All three seeds then return to their original position.)

NARRATOR: When anyone hears the Word of the Kingdom without understanding, the evil one comes and carries off what was sown in their heart. This is the person who received the seed on the edge of the path.

(ACTION: The centre person in GROUP B stands, steps forward, then stands with feet apart, head erect, and arms to the side. S/he then bows his/her head slightly.)

NARRATOR: The one who received it on patches of rock is the person who hears the word and welcomes it at once with joy. But they have no root in them, and they do not last; let some trial come or some persecution on account of the Word, and they fall away at once.

(ACTION: The centre person in GROUP C stands and assumes the same position as B. They then bow their heads.)

NARRATOR: The one who received the seeds in thorns is the person who hears the word, but the worries of this world and the lure of riches choke the word and so they produce nothing.

(ACTION: The centre person in GROUP D stands in the same manner as B and also bows his/her head.)

NARRATOR: And the one who received the seed in rich soil is the person who hears the word and understands it.

(ACTION: The centre person in GROUP F stands and assumes the same position as the other standing people.)

NARRATOR: They are the ones who yield the harvest and produce now a hundredfold, now sixty, now thirty.

(ACTION: The last person to stand [i.e., the person in GROUP F] turns to face the sower. SOWER beckons the person to come to him/her. SOWER places his/her hand on the persons shoulder and they turn together to face with their backs to the audience.)

NARRATOR: And this is the Good News of the the Lord.

Parable of
the Talents

The purpose of the next two mimes is to stay as close as possible to the original text so that the mimes can be used in any setting, from educational to liturgical. At the same time I have no desire to be literal in my interpretation of the parables, so the movement is stylized to present the image rather than each word. Some of the movements (e.g., the increasing money or talents, the planting of the seeds and their growth) are meant to be humorous. This was my intention as I am convinced that the handing on of faith through stories need not be a dreary affair. Much of the movement is set out; some is left to the reader to interpret. The numbers in groups is flexible. I have only set down a specific number for the purpose of writing. However, I would advise against using too many children as the area and the story would become cluttered.

(OPENING POSITION: The owner, to whom we shall refer from now on as O, is standing, facing the audience, right-front of stage. The numbered children are standing still, facing the front, while the lettered children are standing directly behind them, facing the back. Workers 1, 2, and 3 are off to the left.

*There is only one prop, a blanket, which is on the floor behind
number 8; its use will become apparent later. There is also a
narrator. The whole scene should look something like this:*

          Blanket

      8   F G   A B C D E
                     6 7   1 2 3 4 5

W3 W2 W1
                                O

NARRATOR: The Kingdom of Heaven is like the owner of a
large estate who had to go away on business. So he summoned
his workers to him.

*(O beckons to the first worker, who proceeds across from
the left to O. They stand facing one another and shake hands
as the narrator reads,)*

NARRATOR: To the first worker he gave fifty dollars.

*(O points to the first group and the worker goes and stands
beside them:)*

                F G   A BCDE
          8   6 7   W1 1 2 3 4 5

W3 W2   O

NARRATOR: To the second worker he gave twenty dollars.

(The second worker proceeds across from the left to O. They stand facing one another, they shake hands, and he proceeds to the side of his group.)

NARRATOR: To the last he gave ten dollars.

(The third worker moves across to O and repeats the same action as worker 1 and 2.)

NARRATOR: Then the owner left them.

(O turns his back to the audience and moves up-stage to a position behind all the groups and freezes with his back to the audience.)

<pre>
              O
      F G   A BCDE
W3 8   W2 6 7   W1 1 2 34 5
</pre>

NARRATOR: Now the first worker worked and worked with all his money.

(The worker busies himself around his group, perhaps dusting it, etc. Then he takes the arms of the two end children and moves them slowly up and down in unison in a pumping action. When he lets go of their arms they continue to move by themselves. Then he proceeds to the other end of the line and does likewise as the narrator reads,)

NARRATOR: Soon his money began working for him and before long, *POP!*[1]

(On the POP, the front-numbered line bobs down still facing the audience, while the back-lettered line turns, still standing, to face the audience. All the children and the worker are smiling brightly. All freeze.)

NARRATOR: His fifty dollars had become one hundred. In the same way the second worker worked and worked with his money.

(The second worker repeats the action of the first with his group.)

NARRATOR: Until *POP!* his twenty dollars had become forty.

(Same as with the last group.)

NARRATOR: But the man who had received ten dollars dug a hole in the ground and covered his money up.

(The last worker looks around in a worried manner to the right and to the left, then he pushes his money down into a crouching position and covers the money with a blanket. He then stands directly in front of the covered money with his hands behind his back and mimes whistling, looking around as if nothing has happened.)

NARRATOR: Then after a long time the owner returned.

(O turns and walks forward from the rear and proceeds across to the worker with the first group.)

```
        F G       A B C D E
W3 8   W2 6 7   W1  1 2 3 45
                 O
```

NARRATOR: The worker who had received fifty dollars said, "Sir, you gave me fifty dollars to work with and look, here is fifty dollars more."

(*O, the worker, and the money all smile broadly, obviously pleased.*)

NARRATOR: The owner said, "Well done, you good and faithful worker, you have shown that you can be trusted with small things, so I will trust you with much more. Go and wait for me in my Kingdom."

(*O motions to the first worker to go and stand in O's opening position. As he goes, his "money" applauds him politely. O proceeds to the second group.*)

NARRATOR: The worker who had received twenty dollars said, "Sir, you gave me twenty dollars to work with and see, here is twenty dollars more."

(*ACTION: Same as above.*)

NARRATOR: The owner said, "Well done, good and faithful worker, you have shown that you can be trusted with small things, so I will trust you with much more. Go and wait for me in my Kingdom."

(*ACTION: Same as above.*)

NARRATOR: But the last worker said, "Sir, I knew that you were a hard man and I was afraid, so I hid the money you gave me and here it is."

(*The last worker removes the blanket and very slowly up bobs his money, obviously very much the worse for wear. O is not amused.*)

NARRATOR: The owner was very angry and said, "So you knew that I was a hard man and you were afraid. But I tell you, because of your fear, everything I gave you has been wasted. Now, because of your fear, even the little you had is now useless and you are left nothing. So, go from my sight and never return."

(O goes over to other workers and stands between them with his arms on their shoulders as the narrator reads,)

NARRATOR: And the owner and the workers who had served him faithfully all lived and worked together happily ever after.

NOTES

1. **POP:** There are lots of ways to make this sound; use your imagination.

The Wheat and the Darnel

This interpretation of the parable of the wheat and the darnel comes with only slight alterations from the Gospel of Matthew 13:24-30. It requires 13 players and a narrator. One player will be the owner of the estate, one will be his enemy, and another will be his servant. The other ten players are divided into five wheat seeds and five weed seeds.

(OPENING POSITION: Owner, who will be referred to from here on as O, is standing facing the audience. The seeds and the weeds are crouching, facing the audience. The servant [S] and enemy [E] are standing up-stage-left with their backs to the audience. The whole picture should look like this:)

S E

    1   A

5 2   O   F B

  43   D C

NARRATOR: He put another parable to them. "The Kingdom of heaven may be compared to a man who sowed good seed in his field."

(O goes over to the wheat seeds and one at a time brings them to centre stage and places them around the centre stage. Now the scene should like this:)

```
        S   E


    3     2          A
        O         F  B
        1         D C
    4     5
```

(O looks around at his handiwork, smiles, rubs his hands together, and proceeds down stage to the left front. He drops his head and freezes to indicate "sleep.")

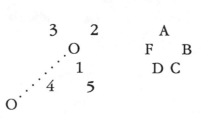

```
        S   E


    3     2          A
        .O        F   B
        . . 1         D C
      .. 4     5
   O.
```

NARRATOR: While everyone was asleep, his enemy came and sowed weeds among the wheat.

(E turns to face the audience, skulks forward from the back, and looks around at the owner's newly sown seed in a most menacing manner. Then one at a time, he sows weeds in among the wheat. So now the stage area looks like this:)

```
      S

           3    F   B
           C    E    2
         4        1   A
             D    5
      O
```

NARRATOR: The enemy made off.

(Exit E by right—E's exit should be suitably melodramatic. O awakes, yawns, stretches, and then turns side on to watch the wheat grow.)

NARRATOR: When the new seeds sprouted and ripened,

(Seeds grow up with big smiles on their faces. The owner looks pleased.)

NARRATOR: the weeds appeared as well.

(Weeds grow up with nasty scowls on their faces. The owner looks anything but pleased.)

(*O moves to centre front and looks around at the mess; he is annoyed. S turns to face the audience and proceeds forward through the weeds and the wheat with shock written all over his face. He proceeds to centre front to face the owner. So the whole picture should look like this:*)

```
        3       F     B
        C                   2
                1     A
        4 D           5                        OS
```

NARRATOR: The owner's servants went to him and said, "Sir, was it not good seed that you sowed in your field? If so, where does the weed come from?" "Some enemy has done this," he answered. And the servants said to him, "Do you want us to go and weed it out?" But he said, "No, because when you pull out the weeds you may pull out the wheat as well."

(*During this narrative the servant and the owner can make simple gestures to emphasis the words. I will not attempt to write them out here as any simple gestures will suffice.*)

NARRATOR: "Let them grow until harvest time and during the harvest I will say to the reapers: first collect the weeds and tie them in bundles."

(*At this the servant gathers up all the weeds and takes them across centre right and bunches them close together. The stage looks like this:*)

NARRATOR: "Then collect the wheat."

(*The servant gathers up the wheat and takes them to the centre. Thus:*)

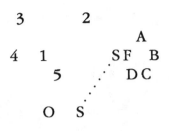

(*The owner makes a strong gesture toward the weeds as the narrator reads,*)

NARRATOR: "The weeds shall be burnt."

```
    1                   A
  5 2                   F  B
  43 S . . . . . . . . S  D C

       O
```

(*The weeds all shrivel up in a heap. Then the owner and the servant go over and join the wheat as the narrator reads,*)

NARRATOR: "And the wheat shall be gathered together into my barn."

(*Owner, servant, and wheat stand in a circle and place their arms over each others shoulders, thus:*)

```
    1                 A
  5   2               F  B
  O   S               D C
    43
```

Christmas Mime

The mime itself is short and simple and is based on Matthew 25:35-46.

You will need to have one person who will be the central figure of the mime as well as four groups of people, perhaps three or four people in each group.

Each of the groups should dress in ordinary clothes. One group can be dressed as children with lots of toys. A second group can be a family with boxes and boxes of giftwrapped Christmas presents. A third group can be a group of women dressed in good clothes and the last group can be a group of partymakers with hats, balloons, and whistles. They will also need a large sign that reads CHRISTMAS. This sign will later be hung around the mimist's head.

I see the main mimist dressed as a clown, but this is entirely up to you.

The mimist enters the sanctuary and looks around. From the expressions on his face, the congregation can see that he is not very happy. From his movements we learn that he is hungry and lonely. He sits down upon the steps of the sanctuary (if there are any) and huddles into a tiny ball.

The first group of people enter the scene. From their clothes we can see that they are a group of children carrying toys. They are laughing and having fun. They come to a still position and freeze. The mimist, startled, looks up at them. He then faces the congregation with a puzzled look on his face. He once again looks at the children. He walks very, very carefully over to the group and peers at them. He then walks around the group, occasionally looking at the congregation.

The group unfreezes and begins to play with their toys, still laughing. The mimist tries to join in the group at play, but each time he is pushed away. He tries several times and each time is rebuffed by the group. At last he gives up and goes back to his original position on the step. Still laughing, the group of children skips off and, as they pass the mimist, they turn their heads obviously the other way.

A few seconds pass and the second group enters. This is the family group. They have been Christmas shopping with the children. Each member of the family is laden down with many presents giftwrapped in brightly coloured paper. Perhaps even one member may have a Christmas tree under one arm. They stop and stand in a group and start to sing carols.

The mimist, upon hearing their voices, raises his head and looks in their direction. He stands and once again very, very slowly goes over to the group and walks around them, occasionally looking at the congregation.

The mimist then bends down on one knee and begs for some food or money from the group. They look at him, turn their heads the other way, and continue to sing their Christmas carols. The mimist gets up and tries from another direction to gain their attention. Once again the family looks at him, then turns away. At last the leader of the group suggests that they move on and so they do. The mimist is left alone. And once again he goes back to his original position.

A few seconds pass and the third group enters. This is the group of partymakers. It is obvious that they are going to a party. They have many different coloured balloons, party hats on their heads, streamers draped around their bodies and whistles in their mouths. They stop and freeze. Once again the mimist goes over to the group very, very slowly. He stops and looks at them as before. He circles the group, occasionally looking at the congregation. Once again he tries to convey to the group that he is lonely and hungry but they too, like the last group, turn their heads and face the other way. The mimist tries several times but each time he is ignored by the partymakers. At last he gives up and goes back to a sitting position.

After a few seconds the partymakers suddenly see him. Laughing and making rather a large noise, they run over to to where the mimist is sitting. They skip around him in a circle and make fun of him. At last one of the partymakers hangs a large sign on the mimist, which reads CHRISTMAS. They skip around him a few more times, making fun of him, and then they run off.

The mimist is very upset. He looks at the congregation. He then very slowly looks at the sign hanging around his neck. He points out each letter of the word carefully. He then looks at the congregation as if to say "What is Christmas?" He stands and takes the sign off from around his neck and walks over to where one of the toys from the first group has been left and puts the sign on the floor near the toy. "Is this Christmas?," he asks the congregation.

He then moves over to where one small Christmas present has been left lying on the floor. Once again he asks the congregation the same question. He finally goes over to where some streamers from the party group have been left, and he picks them up. He asks the congregation the same question again. He shakes his head and walks around the sanctuary looking lost. He then looks up and notices the cross hanging in the church. He goes up to it and places the sign at the foot of the cross or in view of the congregation. He then slowly walks off the sanctuary.

At the conclusion of the mime, a person from the congregation comes up and reads the passage of scripture from Matthew 24:35-40 and 42-46.

The Adulterous Woman

This interpretation of the story of the adulterous woman combines drama, music, and congregational participation. It is designed to be part of a Reconciliation service. Musicians will need to choose a suitably reflective musical setting for the Kyrie[1]. It is important that the prayers and the music are harmonious, so this will need to be practiced.

The reader will be president of the service and as such will not only proclaim the prayers but will represent Christ.

The only thing that will need to be practiced with the congregation is the use of the placard. The placard holder explains that the sign will be used at various stages throughout the service. S/he will have to get the congregation "warmed up" to use the placard.

Lighting should be low, if possible, with only the sanctuary area lit.

For this drama you will need:

A Reader
Three Dramatists
Musicians
A placard with the words STONE HER

Someone to hold the placard
A congregation

READER: (*standing in the centre of the sanctuary*) The Scribes and the Pharisees brought a woman along who had been caught in the very act of committing adultery.

(*Two people drag the accused forward from the rear of the church through the congregation. The accusers throw the accused toward the feet of the reader, they step back a pace and gesture angrily toward her. They then freeze in this position.*)

READER: They said to Jesus, "Master, this woman was caught in the very act of committing adultery."

(*PLACARD HOLDER holds up the sign.*)

CONGREGATION: STONE HER!

READER: "Master, Moses has ordered us in the law to condemn women like this to death by stoning."

(*PLACARD HOLDER holds up the sign.*)

CONGREGATION: STONE HER!

READER: "Jesus, master, what shall we do?"

(*PLACARD HOLDER raises and lowers the sign three times, each time the congregation responds.*)

CONGREGATION: STONE HER! STONE HER! STONE HER!

READER: And Jesus said, "Let anyone who has not sinned cast the first stone."

(Pause, silence. After a brief period of silence the music of the Kyrie begins but it is not sung as yet.)

READER: Father, how quick we are to accuse. How quickly we point out the failings of our brothers and sisters. For the times I have judged others for their weakness, Lord have mercy.

CONGREGATION: LORD HAVE MERCY.

READER: Father, as Christians we can often feel that we are in some way above the rest of humanity and appointed to judge their actions. We are not, and if we are guilty of this, Lord have mercy.

CONGREGATION: LORD HAVE MERCY.

READER: Father, if I have used my position within the church as a place of power or as a pedestal from which I weigh up the actions of my brothers and sisters, Lord have mercy.

CONGREGATION: LORD HAVE MERCY.

(Here the music swells and we sing the Kyrie together.)

READER: And Jesus said, "Go, be at peace with yourself, your neighbours, and your God and sin no more."

CONGREGATION: AMEN

(The music to the Kyrie continues as the congregation makes its final prayer and files out.)

NOTES

1. One suitable "Kyrie" ("Lord Have Mercy") is by Dan Schutte from the album Neither Silver Nor Gold, Phoenix, AZ: North American Liturgy Resources, 1974. The music can be found on page 73 of the book by the same name. It is also available on cassette tape, vol. 2.

From Death to Life

(*for Biddy*)

As the rain begins to fall
And once again caress
The face of this dry earth
To entice from it new life,
In unspoken accord
A single strand of crystal
Leaps from the heart
Of the arid soil
And comes forth to greet the rain.
Life meets life and in their union
They swell and give birth to a stream
Which they bid travel
From the mountains to the sea.
So long alone it stumbles
Over rocks and rough brown earth
Each pebble, each lump of clay
Draws from the stream some moisture
And bit by bit its life
Is drawn out along the way.

But all around the green
Proclaims the water's way
From the corners of the land
Come other streams and rivers
Which are searching for the sea.
Life meets life and once again renewed
They find strength
To continue on their way
Until at last
When all that they can do
For this land is done
One river meets the sea.
Life meets life and then becomes
The fullness of its Word.

Sower and the Seed (2)

(*This is a mime for one performer.*[1])

PROPS:
A large bag
Five signs, each with one of the following words: SEEDS, CLAY, SANDY, THORNS, RICH SOIL
A Bible

The mimist enters and faces the audience. By his/her gestures s/he invites the audience to listen and watch. S/he then looks around the performing area and sees a large potato sack in the corner. S/he asks the audience what is in the bag. S/he then goes over to the right of the performing area and drags back to the centre the large heavy sack.

S/he opens the bag and looks in, occasionally giving a cheeky grin to the audience, as s/he is the only one who knows what is inside the bag. Very, very slowly from the sack s/he pulls out a heavy sign that displays the word SEEDS. S/he gets up and shows this sign to the audience, holding it up with great difficulty for all to see. S/he gestures toward the audience, inviting them to read what is written on the sign. Finally s/he takes the sign and places it to one side.

Walking back to the bag, s/he places his/her hand well inside of it and very slowly produces some imaginary seeds. S/he proceeds to scatter the seeds in one small section of imaginary soil. S/he then begins to water the seeds very slowly.

Once this is done, s/he channels the sun's rays down upon the seeds. Finally, dusting him/herself off, s/he sits down cross-legged in front of them and waits patiently with a smile on his/her face. After a few seconds s/he looks at his/her wrist (time) and back at his/her seeds again. S/he then stands and paces backwards and forwards glancing every now and then at the seeds. By this time his/her facial expression should have changed so that the audience is aware that s/he is growing impatient. S/he then faces the audience and poses the question, "Why won't the seeds grow?" The mimist has an idea and goes back to the seeds and picks up a few grains of soil and lets it sift through his/her fingers. His/her face grows sad as s/he makes his/her way back to the sack.

Putting his/her hand into the sack s/he produces another sign, which reads CLAY. The mimist shows this sign to the audience. S/he places the sign upon the lifeless seeds.

S/he then goes back to the sack and brings out some more imaginary seeds. S/he scatters these seeds in another patch of soil. In the same manner s/he waters them and channels the sun's rays down upon them. This time s/he falls asleep. After a few moments s/he opens one eye and then the other. His/her expression changes to one of astonishment as s/he indicates the seeds are growing and growing. S/he kneels in front of the growing seeds and looks at them lovingly. *Suddenly*, s/he indicates that they have fallen over. S/he tries to make them stand up straight again but they continue to fall over. Once again s/he faces the audience and asks, "Why?" S/he goes back to the seeds and picks up a grain of soil and lets it sift through his/her fingers. S/he shakes his/her head and reaches into his/her sack only to pull out another sign, which reads SANDY. S/he displays this to the audience and places it on the seeds.

Now s/he plants a third patch of seeds. Once again s/he goes through the motions of watering the seeds and channeling the sun's rays onto them. S/he then indicates to the audience that more water may be needed. S/he goes to the side of the performing area and fills his/her imaginary bucket with water.

As s/he returns s/he looks at his/her seeds and finds that they are growing but at the same time they are slowly being choked by thorns. To show this, the mimist places his/her hands around his/her own neck to indicate being choked. A certain amount of over- dramatizing is needed at this point. Finally, s/he stops and looks at his/her seeds and weeps. S/he then pulls from the sack another sign, which reads THORNS. S/he shows this sign to the audience and places it upon the seeds.

Once again the mimist goes to his/her sack and brings out some more seeds. Again s/he plants them, waters them, and channels the sun's rays down upon them. S/he then takes up a cross-legged position in front of the seeds and waits. After a few seconds the seeds begin to grow, and grow, and grow. The mimist indicates this by starting in a crouched position and s/he him/herself grows and grows until finally s/he shows that the plants have grown taller than him/herself. S/he stands back and looks proudly at his/her crop. S/he moves over to his/her sack and takes out another sign, which reads RICH SOIL. S/he displays this sign to the audience and places it next to his/her crop.

The mimist goes back to his/her sack and looks in. S/he indicates to the congregation that there is still one item left in the sack. S/he proceeds to gently lift out the Bible. S/he holds it up high and then brings it in close to his/her chest. S/he indicates to the audience that when they hear the Word of God are they like the SANDY soil, the CLAY soil, the THORNS, or the RICH SOIL.

The mimist then gathers his/her potato sack and leaves the performing area.

NOTES

1. The scripture passage can be read before or after the mime performance, but the mime is preferably performed without any reading.

The Woman with the Haemorrhage

The woman with the haemorrhage (Luke 8:40-48) is yet another miracle story where we read of the healing power of Jesus. Jesus' cure of the woman is a response to her deep faith. He senses the woman's desire to be made clean and whole. His gentleness and concern give the woman courage to step forward and speak.

PROCESS OF REFLECTION

You will read the following process to your group:

Begin by finding your own space on the floor. Start by walking around in a clockwise direction. Walk freely around the room at your own natural pace. Keep walking around. Now walk slowly, very slowly, slower and slower. Now walk quickly, faster and faster. Now gradually slow down until you are walking at your natural pace again. Now begin to walk with large steps, larger and larger still. Now small steps, smaller and smaller. Now come back to your natural walk.

Now as you continue walking around the room, feel your body becoming stiff and tense, stiffer and stiffer. Keep walking but be aware of how difficult it is to move around the room freely. Be aware of how uncomfortable it is to move. In what part of your body does it hurt most? Now slowly begin to let all the tense feeling flow out of you as you continue walking. Change directions as you walk if you feel like doing so. Feel the stiffness flowing out of your body. Now begin to walk at your own natural pace again. Swing your arms as you go. Feel loose and free now back at your natural walk.

Slowly bring yourself to a stop and sit down and relax. You may wish to lie flat on your back. Whatever position you choose, make sure it is a comfortable one for you. Now listen to scripture. (Read the story of the woman with the haemorrhage, Luke 8:40-48.)

(Pause.)

Stand up slowly and find your own space again. I am now going to tell the story again, but in a different way. This time you will only hear the verbs in the story and as you do, reflect for a moment on the word and then embody it.[1]

(As you read the words, do so slowly so as to give people time to embody them fully and also to feel the word. The way that you read the words helps to create an atmosphere for reflection:)

came
touched
stopped
denied
pushing
gone
seeing
discovered
trembling

falling
explained
cured
restored
go

REFLECTION

Once again find your own space to sit or lie in and take a comfortable position. Relax.

As I go through some of the words again, reflect on each of them in terms of your own experiences.

Touched: When was the last time you were touched by someone or something? What people have been touched by you?

Denied: Recall any experience you may have of being denied.

Seeing: How do people see you?

Trembling: When in your life have you been frightened?

Cured: Are you in need of healing in any part of your body right now? Is there perhaps something at this moment that is separating you from God? Bring it to mind and dwell with it for a moment.

Stand slowly and, still reflecting on the part of you that requires healing, decide what part of your body is being crippled. Is it the hand, the back, the heart? Embody it. Now move slowly around the room in this crippled position. Feel whatever is crippling you or hurting you. Feel your body tense and anxious. Now slowly begin to unwind, but keep walking around the room slowly. As you walk, uncurl your body, letting go of all the hurt, of all the pain that is separating you from God. Keep uncurling and walking until you are upright and tall. Begin to walk freely and naturally around the room and listen to these words of scripture:

"Come to me all you who are weary and heavy burdened...and
I will give you rest."

NOTES

1. Embody: to assume a bodily position/gesture that expresses the
word for you.

Peace
on Earth

This narrative mime comes with few directions. It is important for each group of performers to approach the mime freshly and not rehash someone else's interpretation of the script. The places for movement are natural and allow for many interpretations. My only directions highlight when props are to be used. I would also suggest that the movements in the first part of the mime need to incorporate humour in order to heighten the shock of the conclusion.

CAST:
A Narrator
Two Mimists

PROPS:
A Stick
A Slingshot (this could be mimed)
A Cap Gun or Starter's Pistol

NARRATOR: Once there were two neighbours. They were the best of friends. (*As narrator speaks, the two mimists act out his/her words.*)

They worked together.

They played together.

Then one day, one of them invented a new game. He called it arm wrestling. He decided to challenge his friend to the game.

They fought and fought, until the one who had invented the game won.

He was delighted. He told his friend not to worry about losing and that in life someone was always superior. It was called "Survival of the Fittest."

Now his neighbour was very upset at having lost. So, she decided to invent an improvement on arm wrestling. Soon she invented boxing. She practiced and practiced, and before long she was ready to show boxing to her friend.

Well the one who had started the game was concerned. Arm wrestling was one thing, but this boxing was dangerous—a person could get hurt. His neighbour explained that she had merely further developed his original idea. It was the way society traditionally bettered itself. It was called "Progress."

The instigator of the game decided to invent something more advanced than boxing. Something that would make him once again superior. Soon he had the answer, and he went to see his friend. *("A" mimist hits "B" mimist with a stick.)*

There can be no doubt, the results were devastating. Yet surely this was a departure from the rules of the game, said his friend.

The instigator of the game explained that he called this development a "Weapon." *("A" points to stick.)*

His neighbour decided to find a better type of weapon: a weapon that would demand respect, a weapon that would inspire fear.

Before very long, she had found what she was looking for, and she went to let her neighbour see it. *("B" mimes slingshot and lets "A" have it between the eyes.)*

This undoubtedly was a superior weapon. But this was now going beyond a game. His friend reminded him once again that she had not begun the game, she had merely improved upon the original idea. She called it "Escalation."

Now the instigator of the game became angry. He had begun the game. He had won the first contest. Surely this proved that he was superior, but he could not stop now. He would have to find an even better weapon, a weapon so destructive that it would end the game.

He worked and worked on his idea, and eventually he had what he was searching for. He went to show his neighbour. *("A" takes out the gun and shoots "B.")*

That was it. He had finished the game and he had won. He had won.

But, who would he tell?

Our Holy Ghost

There is a ghost inside this man,
That struggles to be free.
It cannot see or hear or speak
And it has no name.

Arms and legs we share
And apart from colour, eyes and hair,
We all look much the same.
Yet our ghosts create the difference,
Our ghosts make us, alone.

They long to find expression,
They long to be laid bare.
They long to speak to other ghosts
And find some comfort there.

My ghost moves me when I dance
And fills me when I sing,
In poetry it finds a voice,
In drama finds its sting.
In art you see its colour,

The clown shows you its face,
But in all these, only glimpses
For the ghost cannot be placed.

There is a ghost inside this man,
That struggles to be free.
It is what I would share with you,
My humanity.

Miss Wombat's Christmas

The Sun came up as usual and shone through the trees of the forest, filtering brilliantly down till it touched the soft, ferny floor below. The animals one by one began to awaken and open their doors and windows to greet the new day. Miss Wombat got out of her warm, snug bed and put on her bright pink dressing gown and her soft, fluffy pink slippers. She made her way down the long tunnel of her burrow to her kitchen where she put on her kettle to brew her morning cup of tea. A whistle blew.

"Ah," thought Miss Wombat, "the postman is here."

Up she went once again through the tunnels, first left and then right until she came to a large door. Opening it, she made her way along the short path, which was bordered by rows and rows of pansies, until she came to her letterbox, an old boot that had been discarded by humans at the local picnic ground.

Miss Wombat opened her letterbox and peeked inside, and there lying on the bottom was a piece of paper neatly folded over four times. Slowly she lifted the paper and opened it to see what it had to say.

CHRISTMAS SALE! was written across the paper in bold black letters. "Christmas Sale," thought Miss Wombat. "What is Christmas?" Quickly she made her way back to the door of her burrow (at least, she moved as fast as a wombat can, which is not very fast at all). She made her way along the tunnel once more and finally back to the kitchen where she found her kettle boiling furiously. She made herself a cup of tea and a slice of toast with honey and sat herself down at the table to look once again at the paper that read CHRISTMAS SALE!

As she drank her tea and munched on her toast and honey, Miss Wombat began to think about Christmas.

"I wonder what Christmas is?" she thought. Seeing that Christmas was on sale and also that she had saved some money, which she kept in an old Twinings Tea tin on top of her kitchen cupboard, she decided that there was no reason why she could not own a Christmas.

After finishing her breakfast, Miss Wombat made her way back to her bedroom where she exchanged her pink dressing and pink slippers for a bright dress and pretty white cap. She placed her purse with her money in it into a basket and made her way up the tunnel once again to the front door and out onto the path.

Miss Wombat had not been walking down the forest road for very long when she met Miss Wallaby, who was sitting at the side of the road munching on some long, green grass.

"Hello Miss Wallaby," said Miss Wombat. "And how are you today?"

"I feel fine, and yourself?" came the reply.

Miss Wombat thought carefully: Should she tell Miss Wallaby about Christmas being on sale or not? After all, when there is a sale, all sorts of animals come from miles around, and Miss Wombat wanted to be sure that there would be enough

Christmas left for her to buy when she got there. But on the other hand, Miss Wallaby was a friend and Miss Wombat did want to share this special news of the sale with her.

"Miss Wallaby," began Miss Wombat, "I am going to a sale— I am going to buy a Christmas; do you want to come with me?"

"WHAT?" replied Miss Wallaby. "What did you say?"

So Miss Wombat told her story of how she found the paper that read CHRISTMAS SALE neatly folded in her letterbox and how she wanted to go and purchase some Christmas before it sold out.

Miss Wallaby began to laugh. She laughed and laughed so hard that her sides hurt. Miss Wombat's feelings were hurt. What was wrong with wanting to buy a Christmas, she thought. So off she went and left Miss Wallaby still laughing at the side of the forest road. Miss Wombat kept on going down the road, singing to herself as she went, "Dum dee dum dee dum." Miss Wallaby's reaction would not deter her from attending the Christmas Sale. She was not going to be put off.

After walking awhile in the hot sun, Miss Wombat decided to rest for a moment on the side of the forest road. She took off her pretty white cap and wiped her brow with the dainty linen handkerchief. As she rested she heard a noise just above her in the high branches of a gum tree. Getting to her paws, she peered up high, only to find Mr. Kookaburra peering down at her.

"Ha ha ha ha hallo Miss Wombat and what brings you out today?" Miss Wombat thought once again. Should she tell Mr. Kookaburra where she was going? After all, he could fly to the Christmas Sale and get there much faster than her. What would she do if he bought all of Christmas and left none for her? But he was her friend and she would like to share Christmas with him.

So she said, "I'm going to buy a Christmas; there's a sale, you know. Look." Miss Wombat began to show Mr. Kookaburra the piece of paper she had found in her letterbox.

"You're going to buy Christmas?" he said, looking at Miss Wombat with gleaming eyes.

"Yes," said Miss Wombat. "Would you like me to buy some for you while I'm there?"

Mr. Kookaburra found it very difficult to keep a straight beak, and slowly he began to laugh, louder and louder until his laugh could be heard all over the forest. He could not stop laughing. He laughed so much that he almost fell out of the huge gum tree.

"How rude," thought Miss Wombat, and she placed her white cap firmly back on her head, picked up her small basket, and continued on her journey.

Time was getting on; the day was nearly over and Miss Wombat decided that she must walk a little faster in order to make the sale before the end of the day. It is difficult for a wombat to walk very fast, but sheer determination to make the sale helped her to put on the speed.

She had walked a fair distance now and was leaving the main forest road to cut across country. This, she thought, was a good idea and would help her to make up some of the lost time. She crossed the little golden bridge that covered the forest waterhole and made her way through the long, lush, green grass before entering another part of the forest. Here tall trees loomed all around. The sun was not as strong as it had been in the morning, and Miss Wombat felt a cold shudder run through her little, round body.

Making her way quickly along a narrow path, Miss Wombat caught sight of Mr. Possum sitting high above in the branches of a tall tree. Mr. Possum was an unusual possum: he didn't have a tail (but that's another story).

"Good afternoon, Mr. Possum," called Miss Wombat. "And how are you today?"

"Just fine," came the reply as Mr. Possum began to climb to a lower branch and then to another low branch until he landed safely on the ground beside Miss Wombat.

"And where are you going?" inquired Mr. Possum.

Now Miss Wombat was worried. Should she tell Mr. Possum about her plans to buy a Christmas? After all, she had been hurt when Miss Wallaby and Mr. Kookaburra laughed at her. No, she decided she would not tell him; she could not bear another animal laughing at her. But, on the other hand, Mr. Possum was old, Mr. Possum was wise, and above all he was kind. He would not laugh at her; she felt sure of this. In fact he would probably accompany her to the Christmas Sale.

"Mr. Possum, I'm going to buy a Christmas. I found this piece of paper in my letterbox," said Miss Wombat, thrusting the paper enthusiastically into the paws of Mr. Possum. He took the piece of paper and looked at it long and hard, glanced at Miss Wombat quickly, and then looked back at the piece of paper.

After some moments Mr. Possum cleared his throat and spoke. "Miss Wombat, what do you think a Christmas looks like and where is this Christmas Sale?"

"Well, I'm not too sure what a Christmas looks like, but I think I'll recognise it when I see it," replied Miss Wombat.

Mr. Possum began to look worried. He ushered Miss Wombat to a small, nearby clump of grass and invited her to sit down. Clearing his voice again he began to speak in a very serious tone.

"You see, dear Miss Wombat, you can't buy a Christmas—Christmas just isn't for sale. Christmas is that special time when we celebrate the journey made by some of the animals of the forest a long time ago to see a very special baby that had been

He would march and stamp,
And skip and tramp,
And hop and run;
Henry would have such good fun.
Apart from playing with his feet,
Our friend Henry loved to eat.
He would find a large gum tree,
Where he could eat all day for free.
He'd chew and munch,
And suck and crunch,
From breakfast time right through to lunch.
When he had had enough to eat,
He decided it was time to sleep.
He slept and slept,
And when he opened up his eyes,
He had a very rude surprise.
From his front right to his back,
He was wrapped up in a tidy sack.
He pushed and shoved,
And pulled and tugged,
But that tight sack never budged.
Poor Henry was so tired
That he just gave up and cried.
As his tears began to drip,
The tight black sack began to rip, rip, RIP.
Henry's heart was full of glee;
He pushed again and then...was FREE.
But Henry found that he had changed;
His body had been rearranged.
First he noticed he was missing feet,
Though the six he had still looked quite neat.
He certainly was not at all sure
What had happened to the other ninety-four.
And now he was no longer green,

But many colours to be seen.
Along with all these other things,
He soon discovered he had wings!
Henry was not sure why
He had become a butterfly,
But as his wings stretched toward the sun,
He knew his life had just begun.

REPORTER: Good evening. (*Insert your own name here*) reporting for International News from Jerusalem. The Holy City is abuzz tonight with some astounding news. Jesus Christ, recently crucified for crimes against the State, has apparently risen from the dead. Several eyewitnesses have reported seeing Jesus, very much alive, in and around the city. Local authorities have dismissed the claims as yet another attempt by Jesus' band of followers to overthrow the government. The governor of Jerusalem, the Right Honorable Pontius Pilate, was this evening unavailable for comment. Tonight we will attempt to piece together the story of Jesus and try to determine if, in fact, he has truly risen from the dead.

Jesus was apparently no ordinary man. To demonstrate this we have some very interesting people to talk to us. My first guests claim to have known Jesus. (*Enter ten ex-lepers who are obviously shy about being on TV.*) Good evening.

LEPERS: (*all together*) Good evening.

REPORTER: May I ask how you people are related to one another?

LEPER 1: Oh! We were lepers.

REPORTER: (*shocked*) LEPERS!

LEPER 2: But we got better.

REPORTER: Do you mean you were cured? Isn't that a bit unusual?

LEPER 3: Yes, Jesus cured us.

REPORTER: What? Jesus cured your leprosy?

LEPER 4: Yes, that's right.

REPORTER: And then what happened?

LEPER 5: Well, we all went to show the High Priest that we had been cured.

REPORTER: No, no, I mean you became followers of this Jesus to show your gratitude?

LEPER 6: Well, not exactly.

REPORTER: Did you at least say thank you?

LEPER 7: Ummmmmmmm...Actually in the rush we sort of...forgot.

REPORTER: YOU FORGOT!

LEPER 8: (*excitedly*) I didn't...I didn't. I came back to thank him.

REPORTER: That's good...but what about the other nine? When you didn't say thanks, didn't your leprosy come back? I mean, didn't Jesus punish you?

LEPER 9: No, we're still quite healthy.

REPORTER: So you're telling me that even though you didn't have time to say thanks to Jesus, he didn't hold it against you?

LEPER 10: Yes, that's right...he seemed like a decent fellow really.

REPORTER: Thank you. Good evening. (*Lepers file out together, nodding at the camera as they go.*) So viewers, it would seem that Jesus was a man of extraordinary power. My next guest has another amazing story. Good evening. (*Ex-lame man comes bounding around in a most excited manner.*)

EX-LAME MAN: (*leaping, jumping, hopping across the stage area and around the reporter.*) Hi! Hi! Hi!

REPORTER: (*annoyed*) Excuse me, sir, could you please stand still? It ruins the camera angles.

EX-LAME MAN: Oh, I'm sorry, I keep forgetting. I'm still getting used to it, you know.

REPORTER: Used to what?

EX-LAME MAN: Oh! Walking, leaping, running, hopping, galloping, skipping. So many things you can do with your legs.

REPORTER: So you're claiming that until recently you could not walk.

EX-LAME MAN: Yes, that's right. But Jesus fixed that.

REPORTER: Jesus cured you, as well as the lepers?

EX-LAME MAN: Yes, but not only us—all sorts of people, blind men, sick people, all kinds really.

REPORTER: And what did Jesus ask for his cures?

DISCIPLE 1: Well, we told Jesus not to come back—to Jerusalem, that is.

DISCIPLE 2: We knew his life was in danger, that people wanted to kill him.

DISCIPLE 3: But he would not listen. He insisted on returning.

DISCIPLE 4: He said he had a job to do. He said that if he did not come back he would not be obeying his father.

DISCIPLE 5: He often said things like that.

DISCIPLE 6: Yes, no matter what we said we could not stop him.

DISCIPLE 7: So, we all came back. Thomas said we might as well all die together, but it didn't turn out that way.

DISCIPLE 8: No, we ran away.

DISCIPLE 9: There were soldiers—so many of them—they came at night. We were afraid. We ran away.

DISCIPLE 10: I followed them; they took Jesus back to see the High Priest. I waited outside but some people recognised me. I was scared that they would take me too so I said that I didn't even know him.

DISCIPLE 11: I was there when they crucified Jesus. His mother was there and some other women from our group. It was horrible. Yet, even as he died Jesus forgave the people who had killed him; he was like that.

DISCIPLE 12: Then, just the other day, some of the women came to tell us that Jesus was gone from the tomb. Mary Magdelene said that she had seen Jesus, ALIVE.

DISCIPLE 12A: Since then we have all seen him. He IS alive.

REPORTER: So what will your group do now?

DISCIPLE 11A: We're not sure. There are so few of us and we are still frightened.

DISCIPLE 10A: Yes, we will go back into hiding and decide what to do.

DISCIPLE 9A: We must go now before we are caught.

REPORTER: Well, there you have it then, the story of Jesus. At the very least he was a most remarkable man. But the question still remains, has he in fact risen from the dead, or is it just a story made up by his followers? I guess it's up to you. What do you believe? (*Your name*) in Jerusalem for International News.

Study Questions

1. What questions would you have asked: (a) the lepers? (b) the lame person? (c) the pharisees? (d) the disciples?

2. What other people could have been interviewed? Think of three.

3. What would you have asked them?

4. Some of the disciples gave us a clue as to who they were. Who was the disciple who: (a) followed Jesus and then denied he knew him? (b) was at the crucifixion?

5. Class Project: Select a panel of six people: three people defending Jesus and three people speaking against him. There will also need to be an interviewer/chairperson. Give each person three minutes to present their case and alternate between defence and prosecution. After the six panelists have spoken, the rest of the class/studio audience has the right to question the panel or to give their own opinions. I would suggest that the class go into a fair amount of research with the teacher before this exercise to understand why some people would not have appreciated a person like Jesus. This will help to make the prosecution more believable.

She leapt up high into the air,
then fell to earth and fainted there.
Now this was really something new;
the Snark did not know what to do.
It was just a game he played for fun;
he didn't mean to hurt anyone.
"Oh Miss Wombat please don't die!"
the giant Snark began to cry.
The animals soon heard this sound,
and they came from all around.
They saw the wombat lying there,
and the great big Snark in such despair.
It was then that they all understood:
the giant Snark was really good.
Soon the wombat was quite well,
and often she was heard to tell
the tale of her fright in the dark
and how she tamed the mighty Snark.
For the Snark said he would not again
say "Boo!" to all his furry friends.
So if you should hear "Boo!" in the dark,
One thing you'll know; it's not a Snark.

The Useless Tune

On a warm and sunny morning, Melissa, a young and graceful magpie, lifted her wings and felt the breeze ruffle her feathers. After stretching for a moment, she leapt from the telegraph pole where she had spent the night and rushed headlong into the day. She drifted on the breeze; she dove and swooped. The smell of the gum leaves in the warm air cleared her head of the last traces of the night, and she felt that she could see forever. Even though she had left home only the day before, the beauty of the morning washed away any sadness she had felt. She basked in her newfound independence. She felt strong. She was ready to go about the serious business of finding a home of her own.

She remembered her mother's parting words, "Melissa, you must find a tree who is willing to give you a home. Not many trees are kind to magpies. They feel we bring more trouble than good. They believe we have nothing to offer them. But we do, for although the magpie is not the most beautiful of birds, we have a special gift from the Creator. Our gift is our song. When we sing, the sound is like water rushing over stones in a riverbed, and if you listen carefully to our song you can almost hear God singing with us. This is the gift you must offer

from her beak and rippled across the bush like water over stones, and as she sang the creatures of the bush stopped for a moment to hear her song, and those that heard her felt the troubles of the day fall away and they felt refreshed, renewed. When she had finished, Melissa felt sure that the tree would be impressed; after all, she was impressed.

"Nice," said the tree, "but I've got no use for singers. Will your singing stop the termites eating my wood? Will your singing stop the floods from knocking me down? Sorry, you'd just be another burden to carry. It's a tough world, magpie; face it, singers just aren't, well, useful."

Melissa was shattered. She had felt sure this tree would give her a home, especially after he had heard her song, which was considered quite good even by magpie standards. Unfortunately, she could see the logic in the tree's words. She couldn't stop the floods or termites with her singing. She was, after all, useless.

She flew from tree to tree, begging each one to give her a home, but everywhere she went the answer was the same. What use was a singer to anyone? Night came and she flew blindly on, not knowing what was to become of her. Finally her young wings could no longer support her weight and she fell exhausted to the ground, unable to move and not caring what might happen to her. She lay there sobbing until she fell into an unhappy sleep. Night and silence engulfed her.

"Hi there."

Melissa awoke startled. Already the sun was creeping over the horizon. She wondered who had spoken to her.

"Hello, are you alright?"

Melissa raised her tired eyes to see a small and rather shaggy Stringy Bark tree speaking to her.

"What sort of bird sleeps on the ground?" asked the tree.

"A tired one," snapped Melissa.

"Oh," said the tree thoughtfully. "If you are tired, why didn't you ask and you could have spent the night in one of my branches. I've got plenty of room."

Melissa looked the Stringy Bark up and down. It was a very small and rather tatty looking tree. In places its bark had great shaggy-looking strips hanging off it. It was also quite small— hardly large enough to be called a shrub. It wasn't the magnificent home she had once imagined, yet the tree had a friendly look about it and when the wind brushed by its branches it seemed to dance and its leaves chattered and laughed.

Melissa mustered all her courage and blurted out, "Look I don't suppose it would be possible to build a nest in one of your branches would it?"

"Sure," replied the tree, "Do you sing?"

"Well, not any more," answered Melissa. "I gave up."

"Why?" questioned the tree.

"Well," began Melissa, "look at it this way. My singing is not going to bring rain in the drought or prevent you from being cut down, burnt up, being eaten, or drowned in a flood. Singing is no good to anybody. It's, well, it's kinda useless, don't you see."

"I see your point," the tree replied. "Your singing won't stop any of those things from happening. But I've been told, and I have it on very good authority, that when a magpie sings you can almost hear God singing with it. And although you cannot protect me with your singing, it will make things seem better— if something bad should happen. I would very much like to hear you sing. It would make me happy. Would you sing for me now?"

Well Melissa could hardly refuse, so she composed herself, drew a deep breath, and began to sing. As she sang the tree swayed its branches in time to the tune, and the day seemed to smile on the two young creations.

Let your breath come and go as it will; don't hold on to your breath. Don't try to control it in any way; let it just come and go. Be aware of your breath; stay with this awareness for a moment.

Now, keeping your eyes closed, just begin to move, any way at all, just for the sake of moving. You are now waking your body and bringing it to life. Move in all sorts of ways--just for the sake of moving. You need not remain on your back; you can bend, stretch, twist, turn in any way at all. Remember to use your whole body, every part of it. Try moving in all directions. Move in ways that you have never moved before; it doesn't matter what you look like; your eyes are still closed. This is your dance.

The following passage may be read as the movement is taking place.

> Yahweh God, fashioned man from the dust of
> the soil. Then He breathed into his nostrils
> a breath of life and man became a living being.
> (Genesis 2:7)

Repeat the above movement, but as you do so, try to feel your whole body being charged with God's Holy Spirit.

WIND AND FIRE

There is a mystery in the wind, sometimes it is a great, violent force, other times it is soft and gentle. It is the spirit that gives something its life and over which the thing is not master. In a similar way, man is not master to his breathing. Man's breathing comes from God and returns to God at the moment of death.

Once again find a place where you have plenty of room to move around in and take a relaxed position. Close your eyes; get ready to move.

I am going to name some familiar things. I want you to think about each one and how they move.

Wind: move like the wind. If it helps you to move, you may like to make sounds with your voice. Wind has different strengths: sometimes it is soft and gentle like a cool breeze; sometimes it is hard and forceful. Sometimes wind can move in circles. Make some of your movements circular ones; make some movements short and brisk and others long and flowing. Relax.

Fire: think about fire. Imagine a fire; picture it; hear the noise; smell its smell; think about the quality of the movement of the fire. Feel the movement in your muscles and express it in movement. Move as the fire moves. Discover and explore new movements, fiery movements. Sometimes fire is warm, friendly, and playful; sometimes is it wild, violent, and destructive.

The above movements can be repeated but this time in pairs, working together not to create two separate dances, but joining together to create one dance. Increase the size of the group gradually so that all participants are joining together as one body in one dance.

Break the children into groups: some to decorate the room, some to make banners, and perhaps some to blow up balloons. Tell the children that you are preparing the room for the coming of Jesus.

PROMISES

After the preparation of the room is completed, tell the children that the reason you went to so much trouble to make the room look nice was because Jesus is so important. God promised a very long time ago that he would send us Jesus. God made promises to lots of people in the Bible.

Talk with the children about some of these people: Noah, Abraham, David, etc. God always kept his promises to these people, even when some of them did not keep their promises to Him.

Tell the children that because God made us such an important promise in Jesus, perhaps we should make a promise to Him in return.

MATERIALS:
One empty matchbox for each child
Coloured giftwrapping paper
String

Ask the children to write their promise to God for this Christmas on a small piece of paper. They then place their promise inside the small matchbox, wrap the matchbox in the coloured paper, and decorate it however they wish. Make sure when the string is tied onto the matchbox that there is a loop so that it may hang onto the tree. Ask the children to keep their promises in a safe place, for they will be using these to hang on their own Promise Tree during the paraliturgy to follow.

LITURGY

OPENING SONG: (*"Come Lord Jesus" from* Hi God *by Carey Landry. Simple hand gestures could be choreographed for all the children to do during the singing of this song.*)

OPENING PRAYER: Lord, since the beginning of the world you have made people promises. You promised Noah that you would keep him safe from the flood. You promised Abraham and Sarah that you would give them a son. You promised Moses a land where he could take the people of Israel. You promised us that you would send Jesus to be our friend and to show us how to live. You always kept your promise, even when other people did not keep theirs. Today, we would like to say thank you and to make you a promise of our own.

PENITENTIAL RITE: Coming together as God's friends and believing in all His promises, we want to say that we are sorry for the times that we have not kept our promises. God, you promised us your Son to give us peace so that everyone could live as friends; Lord have mercy.

Lord Jesus, you are the Son of God and the Son of Mary; Lord have mercy.
Lord Jesus, you became a baby and were born in a stable; Lord have mercy.
May God be kind to us all, forgive us the things we do wrong, and bring us to live with Him forever. Amen

FIRST READING: (Isaiah 9:5-7)

PSALM: (Psalm 107:1-9)

Response: We thank you, God,

Dancing Carols

The following choreography for the carols was created to be learned and enjoyed by both young and old. The dances take the forms of either circles or lines, which help the dancers to develop even further the sense of community so often felt at Christmas. Here we pick up and renew the traditions of Christian dance during the first twelve centuries where these line and circle dances were common.

The early Christmas carols were divided into two parts: the stanza and the chorus. During the stanza (verse) the dancers stood still while the leader (or the whole group) sang. During the chorus they danced or in some instances danced and sang at the same time.

As these dances are done in a folk style, it is important that the tempo of the music is such that these dances can be performed with energy and gusto.

O COME ALL YE FAITHFUL

This dance requires groups of eight people. They are arranged and numbered in the following way:

```
    1   1
  2       2
  2       2
    1   1
```

O come all ye faithful,

(ONES will take a step forward into the centre of the set on their right foot and hop on it. Step on the left foot and hop on it. Repeat on the right foot and again on the left.

Four step-hops in all. Two into the centre and two back to original position. The two step-hops going backward commence on the right foot.)

Joyful and triumphant.

(TWOS repeat two step-hops into the centre of the set, commencing on right foot and two step-hops backward to original starting position, commencing on the right foot.)

O come ye, O come ye to Bethlehem.

(Face your partner and link left arms. Do four step-hops around in your own circle with your partner going to the right and commencing on your right foot.)

Come and behold Him,

(Facing the centre of the set, take four steps into the centre, starting on the right foot. The body is bent over to begin and gradually comes up on the fourth step with the arms raised up high.)

Born the King of Angels.

(Still facing the centre of the set, take four walking steps backward to original place, commencing on the right foot and bringing arms down to the sides at the same time. Body also comes down into a bow position.)

(Here we re-number the groups like this:)

```
    1   2
 2        1
 1        2
    2   1
```

O come let us adore Him,

(ONES make a right-hand star,[1] skipping for eight counts in a clockwise direction and back to place.)

O come let us adore Him,

(TWOS make a right-hand star, skipping for eight counts in a clockwise direction and back to place.)

O come let us adore Him,

(All make a right-hand star, skipping for eight counts in a clockwise direction and back to place.)

Christ The Lord.

(All raise arms into the centre of the circle with palms facing upward.)

GOD REST YE MERRY GENTLEFOLK

This simple dance is based on skipping. The group looks like this:

1   2

2   1

God rest ye merry gentlefolk,

(Holding hands, the group skips around to the right for eight counts, starting on the right foot.)

Let nothing you dismay.

(Still holding hands, the group skips around to the left by swinging their right foot across their body and beginning their eight skips on the right foot. Drop hands.)

Remember Christ our Saviour

(Facing the centre of the set, ONES skip into the centre to face each other. There are eight skips altogether. Two into the centre, two on the spot, two going backwards to original place and two more on the spot. These commence on the right foot.)

Was born on Christmas Day

(The above movement is repeated by TWOS.)

To save us all from Satan's power

(Facing partner and taking their right hand, skip around to the left for eight counts.)

When we had gone astray.

(*Change hands and skip for eight counts around to the right.*)

O tidings of comfort and joy,

(*All the people in the group take hands, walk around the centre of the circle, and raise hands up high, starting on the right foot. Five walks.*)

Comfort and joy,)

(*Hold position with hands up high.*)

O tidings of comfort and joy.

(*Five walks back to original position, starting on the right foot and hold the arms up in the air.*
Repeat from the beginning as many times as required.)

DECK THE HALLS

This dance requires two lines, and the dancers are numbered thus:

Deck the halls with boughs of holly. Falalalala, lala la la.

```
1   2
1   2
1   2
1   2
1   2
```

(ONES do-si-do^2 around TWOS, passing by their right shoulder. This is a skipping step: eight skips.)

'Tis the season to be jolly. Falalalala, lala la la.

(TWOS do-si-do around ONES, passing by their right shoulders as above.)

Don we now our gay apparel.

(Facing partner opposite, clap right hands twice and clap left hands twice.)

Falala lalala la la la

(Four slip-steps coming down the room, holding both partner's hands.)

Toll the ancient yuletide carol.

(Clap right hands twice and clap left hands twice.)

Falalalala lala la la.

(Four slip steps back to original place, holding both partner's hands.
Repeat as many times as is necessary.)

NOTES

1. **Right-hand star:** This is formed when the group is skipping around in a clockwise direction, their bodies facing the way they are going. Their right hands are placed in the centre as they skip around in a circle.)

2. Do-si-do: Two people face each other. One partner skips around the other partner, passing him/her back to back, and skips backward to his/her original place. S/he passes his/her partner by the right shoulder and comes back to the original starting position by the left shoulder.)

Creative Dance and Psalms

Praise Him with blasts of trumpets
Praise Him with lyre and harp,
Praise Him with drums and dancing
(Psalm 150:3-4)

Psalm 150 is the final psalm in the Psalter. It is believed that this psalm is the work of the compiler of the entire collection. It is a benediction of praise in which the writer calls upon every imaginable instrument of praise to join in their great ovation to God.

Indeed it is fitting that the most beautiful of all instruments—the body—be used to praise and glorify God.

In this chapter I would like to suggest that you ask the children to write their own psalm, a psalm of praise. In their psalm they can mention things that are familiar to them. The next step is to interpret the psalm through creative movement.

The lesson could take the following format:

STEP 1: (*Ask the children if they can tell you anything at all about the psalms. I have left how you will develop this discussion up to you as it will vary according to the age level of the children.*)

STEP 2: Let's look at Psalm 150. What do you think this psalm is about?

- What is it saying?
- What are some of the things mentioned in the psalm?
- What are lyres and harps?

Can you remember any other musical instruments mentioned in the psalm?

What other instruments might the people have used (ram's horns, cymbals, timbrels, animal skin drums, bells, reed flutes)? What do we mean by the word "praise"?

Can you show me a gesture of "praise"?

(*NOTE: Try to encourage the children to find as many gestures as they can to interpret this word. This will avoid them always using the "hands raised to the heavens" gesture.*)

STEP 3: Let's look at verse 2 of the psalm.

Praise Him for His mighty achievements

What are some of His mighty achievements?

Although you may choose any words you like, I have chosen a series of nature words that show us some of these achievements. These words are: water, fire, rain, sun, waves, and wind.

STEP 4: Now we will explore each of these through movement.

Water: (*For this you will need some water in a clear bowl and a tambourine.*) What are some of the words that describe water?

whirling
splashing
rocking
tossing

All of these words suggest some form of movement.

Look at the water in the bowl. See how gentle it is. Stretch your arms out to the sides with your palms facing downward. Keep your arms and your hands very still, just like the surface of the water. Now begin to move them, just a little, very gently, up and down, up and down. Now keep them still again. Repeat this movement several times.

(Ask the children to come and sit around you. Place your hand in the bowl and gently stir the water around until you have made a whirlpool.

Direct the children to find a space of their own to move in, instructing them,)

Now move your whole body like a whirlpool. Use your whole body, every part of you. You may choose to stay on one spot or you may like to move around. Now stop and stand very still. Let's try it again.

How many different ways can you whirl besides going around in a circle? Yes, you can move up and down, maybe one arm and then the other, then both together. Now move your whole body, up and down, up and down. Now combine this movement with a turning movement. Turn slowly at first, then get faster and faster. Now begin to slow down and get slower and slower until you come to a stop.

(Now invite the children to come back together and watch the water in the bowl again. This time your hand splashes the water backward and forward.)

What is the water doing? Yes, splashing backward and forward and from side to side. Let's all stand and once again find our own spot to move in and make splashing movements with our bodies, up and down, side to side. Remember to use all the parts of your body. Make your whole body move.

Now see if you can rock your body gently from side to side.

STEP 5: Now listen to the tambourine. When I shake the tambourine, move your body like a whirlpool. When I beat out the rhythm 1-2-1-2, move your body to show me splashing movements.

(*Here you should vary the rhythm of the tambourine to combine both the shaking and the beating together.*

Slowly bring the tambourine to a stop and invite the children to finish their "water dance" sitting on the floor around the bowl of water.)

STEP 6: (*This could be taken one step further with the use of "chant."*

As the children make their whirling movements, they could add another dimension to their movements by the use of their voice saying over and over,)

"For whirling water, praise the Lord."

(*As the children make their splashing movements, they could say,*)

"For splashing water, praise the Lord."

Fire: (*The word "fire" can also be explored in the same manner. Words that suggest movement are:*)

writhe
twist
shoot
flicker

(Movements such as writhing could begin in one part of the body and extend slowly through to other parts or from one child to another forming a "writhing chain." For an extra effect, crepe paper could be used. This could be cut and used to create a streamer effect.

Once again, the chant can be used to accompany the movement.)

"For flickering fire, praise the Lord."
"For twisting flames, praise the Lord."

Rain: *(This exercise requires a woodblock or tambourine.)* Here we will explore the beating rhythm of the rain as it falls.

(The directions for this movement can be as follows:)

Stand very still and straight with both feet together. Bounce very gently like the rain beating down.

Now try beating with your feet *(accompany with the beating of the tambourine or woodblock.)*

Now sit on the floor and gently beat with your hands. *(Divide the class into two. Direct one side to beat the floor and the other side to clap their hands.)*

Now make silent, beating movements using your whole body, arms, legs, head, and feet.

(Once again the chant can be used to accompany the movements.)

Sun: *(Again ask the children to find their own space to move in. Once they are settled, the directions for this movement can be as follows:)*

Can you imagine the sun rising? What do you see? Perhaps the light, its rays shining as it leaps into the sky.

Everyone sit on the floor. Roll yourself up into a tiny ball. Make yourself as small as you can. Yes, even smaller than that. When you are as small as you can be, slowly begin to unwind and uncurl yourself. Make very slow movements. Begin to rise up slowly until you are in a standing position. Stretch up as far as you can.

Now imagine that you are the sun and that you are shooting heat rays out in all directions. Use both your arms and your legs. Shoot them out with forceful movements. (*Here again streamers can be used for added effect.*)

Now imagine that you are the sun slowly sinking. Begin to shrink and curl yourself up into a small ball, smaller and smaller. Sink until you are back resting on the floor.

(*You can extend this exercise by asking the children to move from place to place, at the same time shooting out their rays in all directions, which would show the sun's rising, its moving from east to west, and finally its sinking in the evening.*

Here the chant will be:)

"For the sun that shines, praise the Lord."

(*The same format can be used for the words "waves" and "wind."*)

Words that suggest movement for waves are "rising," "sinking," "rolling," "crashing," and "thundering."

Explore ways in which parts of your body can rise and sink. How many different ways can you do this?

Make clashing movements with your body bouncing off each other.

Make thunder-like movements with your body. Use your voice as well.

"Clashing waves, praise the Lord."

(*Once again add green, blue, and white streamers.*)

Draw or paint a picture of the patterns of the streamers as they flowed through the air.

Explore each of the following words through bodily movement: "sweep," "sway," "whirl," "fall," "roll," "leap."

(*The chant can be,*)

"For sweeping wind, praise the Lord."

When we put all the chants together we have the following:

Alleluia
For whirling water, praise the Lord.
For flickering fire, praise the Lord.
For beating rain, praise the Lord.
For the sun that shines, praise the Lord.
For clashing waves, praise the Lord.
For sweeping wind, praise the Lord.
For all of nature, praise the Lord.
Alleluia

(There are many other directions that a psalm of praise can take [e.g., For the gift of ourselves, praise the Lord.]

Here we can explore the various parts of the body and how they move [e.g., arms, legs, feet, hands, face, eyes]. Once again, we can go on to create our own psalms.)

Please Be A King This Time

How often have we raised our eyes
and strained to see some sign.
Perhaps another star to guide
your people to a newborn King.
This time a King indeed,
not hidden in ragged cloth
or dimly seen in prophecy,
but a King that's plain to see.
We built this kingdom in our dreams,
but would you sit
in comfort on our throne?
How often have we prayed
for you to come,
in grand defiance of a world
that mocks us for our faith,
and makes them pay the levy
for their disbelief.
No stable this time.
No chance of being misunderstood.

This second time,
would you thunder down
from heavens gates,
throw down the princes of the world,
and stand in glory for all to see?
And would those
who dared to disbelieve,
be cast into dismay?
Would they tremble
in your presence,
blink in your eternal light
and shudder at their foolishness
as they stumble from your path?
Would the world at last admit
that you are Lord
and bow down in your sight?
Do we crave this?
Is this our secret longing?
To see those who called us fools
one day cower at our feet
and beg to be like us.
And will you come again...like this?
Or will there be another Bethlehem?
Another open-ended life
that leaves us in our doubt.
Is this victory or defeat?

Dance
with Infants

The most difficult age group to work with is infants through the ages of five to seven. Good music with simple tunes for this age group is hard to find.

All young children enjoy music and movement. They show signs of creativity and imagination and are able to express this freely by using their bodies to interpret their feelings and to create images.

The child already understands some movement vocabulary (i.e., run, jump, skip, bend, stretch, walk, fall).

For this age group, I find lessons of no longer than twenty minutes are the best.

Here I have outlined three lessons that I have used for younger children. They may be of help to those who are wondering where to begin. These lessons were each twenty minutes. In them I have used some of the elements of creative dance as my approach.

The aim of the lessons is to accomplish the following:

- provide experiences through movements, which will help the child's natural feeling for movement;
- stimulate their imaginations;

- develop an awareness of the body as a means of communication;

- realise that every movement they make and every breath they breathe comes from God and that we are his children:

Yet in fact, He is not far from us,
since it is in Him that we live, and move and exist
for as some writers have said, "We are His Children."
(Acts 17:28-29)

PART ONE: SPACE

Vocabulary: sit, lie, kneel, stand, up, down, back, side, front.

(The first part of this lesson makes the children aware of the room you are in and all the things that are in the room [furniture, people, etc.]).

Find a space in the room where you will have enough room to move around without touching anyone or anything. When you have found this space, sit down.

Now in your own special place, make all kinds of big movement. Remember not to touch anyone or anything; this is your own special space.

(I have found it a great help to children if I begin to do the movement, too, but gradually stopping, allowing them to create movements of their own.)

PART TWO: MOVEMENTS IN RELATION TO THEIR OWN BODY

Now sit down. Lie down; can you lie on your back? Now on your side. Try on your back again; and lastly on to your side. Now sit up slowly.

Now can you kneel up? (*Some little children find keeping their balance in this position difficult.*)

Now let's stand up.

PART THREE: MOVEMENTS IN RELATION TO OTHER CHILDREN

(*Ask the children to sit in a space. Ask one child to walk around the room, being aware of all the other children as well as the furniture in the room, but not touching the other children or the furniture.*

Repeat, asking various children, one by one, to walk around the room.

Now ask all the children to walk around the room, but they must not touch each other or anything else.

Watch the children to see how they are walking. Invite them to walk with their heads up, looking straight ahead.

Invite them to walk as children of God.)

PART FOUR: TIME

Vocabulary: slow, fast.

Here we explore movements in our own place and then movements from place to place.

Movements in our own place:

Let's sit down slowly.
Let's stand up slowly.
Lie down slowly.
Stand up fast.
Sit down fast.

Movements from place to place:

Can you walk fast?.
Now walk slowly.
Can you run fast?.
Now run slowly.

Now you can do whatever movement you like, but you must listen to me to hear whether you should move slowly or fast.
(Here allow the children to choose their own movement but s/he alternates between fast and slow movements.)

PART FIVE: FORCE

Vocabulary: soft, hard, gentle

Can you imagine a leaf floating through the air? *(Invite the children to close their eyes to picture the leaf gently floating down.)*
Can you be a leaf? Yes, make soft movements.
Can you imagine you are stroking a kitten? Show me—yes, soft, gentle movements.
Can you show me any other soft, gentle movements?
Now, can you show me some hard movements? Yes, like punching a bag and clapping your hands.

PART SIX: FREE EXPRESSION

(Here I invited the children to move in any way they wished. They were encouraged to find different ways of moving either on the floor, sitting, standing, or perhaps moving from place to place.)

PART SEVEN: LOOKING AT OUR BODY

In the previous sections we looked at how our body moves as a whole. Now we begin to explore the different parts of our body and how they move (e.g., eyes, fingers, head, hands, toes, feet, trunk, legs).

(At the conclusion of the lessons I chose the tune "Jesus is a Friend of Mine," which can be found in the book Sound of Living Waters *by Betty Pulkingham and Jeanne Harper. I asked the children to help me write the words to the song. This is what eventuated:)*

God gave me hands to clap
He loves me

God gave me hands to clap
He loves me

He loves me
He loves me

God gave me hands to clap
He loves me

(We then went on to:)

God gave me feet to tap...
God gave me eyes to see...
God gave me legs to run...

(As we sang the song, the children responded with appropriate movements to the verses of the song.
At the conclusion of the lesson we finished in prayer.)

Thank you God for our legs to run and walk, to leap and jump with.

Thank you God for our eyes to see all the great things you have made.

Thank you God for my hands to clap, to shake and to touch things with.

But especially God, thank you for me.

Healing through Dance

The number of ways you can express the miracles of Jesus in dance is limited only by your imagination. For the purpose of this chapter, we will deal with only one way: expressing the miracles through creative movement.

When attempting to express the miracles or any other story using creative movement, you should first place yourself inside the situation you wish to interpret; feel the ground beneath your feet and see the scene as it was. Become a part of it, and when you move, interpret what you see. Let the expression flow from within, rather than confining yourself to a set routine.

The story we have chosen as an example is the miracle of the ten lepers from Luke 17:11-19. The movement in this story is from confinement (leprosy) to freedom (health). We will detail first the reflection process and then a visual expression of the story. The first half of the reflection enables us to experience the freedom we already possess in our bodies. From

147

there the second half of the reflection process draws us into the bodies of lepers where we await the freedom Christ will bring.

PROCESS OF REFLECTION

You will need the following:

A tambourine
A Bible
A cleared space large enough to move freely around in.

Find a space in the room; this is your own personal space. Slowly stretch your arms out around you. Feel the space; reach up high; reach out to the sides; reach down low; stretch your whole body and explore every bit of the space the surrounds you, and then relax.

Walk around the room, naturally and at a regular pace. Keep on walking; swing your arms as you walk; keep well away from others. Now with your whole body, walk as slowly as you can; go slower and slower; slow down even further; gradually feel your whole body becoming heavier and heavier; slow right down, and freeze.

Walk around the room again; just walk naturally and at a regular pace. Now slowly begin to quicken your steps: faster, faster, and even faster still.

Now take large steps and begin to slow down to a regular pace again. Make your steps larger and larger—giant steps. Now take small steps—tiny steps—even smaller than you are taking now.

Now take bouncy steps; bounce up and down, up and down as you walk along: bounce, bounce, bounce. Now walk with smooth, even steps: no bounce at all.

Can you walk in a curved path? Now walk in a straight line; walk forward, backward, sideways.

Make up as many original walks as you can. See how many different ways you can walk.

Walk freely again around the room. Keep your whole body straight and your head up. Walk with a spring in your step. Now walk backward again, looking over your shoulder to see where you are going.

As you walk forward again, show how you might walk if you were angry. How would you walk if you were sad? How would you walk if you were bored? How would you walk if you were in pain?

Slowly walk back to your own space and relax.

In your own space, lie flat on your back; feel completely relaxed; let your whole body sink into the floor beneath you. Become aware of your own breathing, in and out, in and out. (At this point, the story of the ten lepers should be read.)

Now take your time and sit up very slowly. What do you know about leprosy? What parts of your body does it strike? How were people warned in Jesus' time that lepers were approaching? Where did this story take place? What was the countryside like? Try to make a mental picture of the countryside. Perhaps the road is hot and dusty. Maybe the sun is beating down upon your back. Feel the warmth of the sun on your face. Place yourself in the picture and stand up slowly.

Imagine that you are a leper: Where has leprosy struck you? Is it in the arm? Or perhaps a leg; maybe it's your back. You may have it in more than one part of your body. Make your body into a twisted shape. Find your own level; you may be standing, you may be crawling, or you may be dragging yourself along the ground. Find your own level. Now make another twisted shape, keeping in mind where leprosy has struck you. How does it feel being a leper? Are you ashamed? How do you think you appear to others? Can you look at others face to face? How do you react when others look at you? Where does it hurt you most of all? Move very slowly, not hurrying at all. Some of you may want to move more slowly than others. How do you communicate with the other lepers? Say something to another leper using gestures only. What are you trying to say?

Putting these movements together and using a tambourine, the scene may look something like this:

A VISUAL EXPRESSION OF THE TEN LEPERS

The reading may be read before or after the expression.

1. Four slow beats of the tambourine

(Lepers enter slowly in their own twisted shapes. They look at their own bodies. Remember to use different levels.)

2. Shake tambourine

(Lepers quickly recoil, hiding their faces.)

3. Four slow beats of the tambourine

(Lepers try to communicate with each other.)

4. Shake tambourine

(Lepers recoil again.)

5. Four slow beats of the tambourine

(Lepers stretch their arms out in all directions: some upward, some out to the sides, some downward.)

6. Shake tambourine

(The lepers recoil again.)

7. Shake tambourine

(Jesus enters.)

8. Shake tambourine

(Lepers look curiously at each other and then at Jesus.)

9. Shake tambourine

(Various expressions of surprise and curiosity cover their faces.

Here we add voices to accompany the movement. Each of the lines are repeated several times for an echo effect, rather like the rhythm of a train.)

Line 1: "Who's coming, who's coming?" (Each of these lines should be repeated four times.)

Line 2: "Who is it?"

Line 3: "Jesus."

Line 4: "Go away."

Line 5: "We're lepers."

Line 6: "Heal us." *(This is said only once and in a loud, sharp, crying voice.)*

(As these lines are spoken, the lepers begin to move in toward each other, closer and closer. Slowly as they come together, they reach out to each other and take hands. The lepers begin to lift up their joined hands and reach out of the group. As they touch each other, they begin to unfold their confined bodies

and become healthy. The group members move out from the group and freeze in attitudes of joy, disbelief, or astonishment. The movement finishes here.)

Another way creative movement can be used with this story is to go through the reflective process and then choose some suitable music and ask the group to improvise the story of the lepers through movement.

In this case the group could experiment with shapes, from twisted, distorted shapes to strong, healthy, whole shapes. (Suitable music for this would be "Oxygene 1" by Jean Michel Jarre.)

You may discover, after your own reflection, a better way of interpreting this story visually. That is the beauty of creative movement: the freedom it allows us.

The Blind Man

The story of the blind man will probably already be familiar to most small children. Here we reflect upon the story using a simple movement and reflection technique.

Sit down on the floor. Now slowly, very slowly, close your eyes; see things becoming fuzzier and fuzzier until you can't see anything at all. Darkness: We all know what it's like to be in the dark, but before there was always some light. But now we are blind and the darkness is all around. Darkness is all we know and all we have known since we were babies. We are blind and our world is dark. We have never seen a flower nor never seen the sun. We don't even know what our parents look like. We can't even imagine what these things look like.

Now slowly stand up. Keep your eyes closed. Stay in your place and turn slowly in a circle to the right until I say stop.

Now very slowly and then very quickly move around the room. Stretch our your hands in front of you. Stretch them out to help you feel your way around, and try not to bump into people and things. Keep your eyes closed. We are blind. Move around for a minute. Stop. Keep your eyes closed. Where are you? Which way are you facing now? What is around you?

Sit down slowly and keep your eyes closed.

We are blind. We have been blind for as long as we can remember. What if we had one wish; what do you think that you would ask for? What do you want to be able to do more than anything? To see?

Keep your eyes closed and I will read a story about a blind man like us and how he came to see.

SCRIPTURE: Mark 8:22-26

This man has been blind for so long he did not believe that Jesus could make him see again. He got so used to being blind that he did not think that he could do anything else. He did not want to be disappointed and he was not sure. That is why the first time that Jesus touched him he only saw a little bit. But that little bit was enough to let him know that if he believed with all his heart, then Jesus would make him see.

What about us? We are blind. Do we believe that Jesus can make us see?

If you believe with all your heart that Jesus can make you see, stretch out your hands in front of you toward Jesus and when you have stretched them out as far as you can, you may open your eyes.

PRAYER: We thank you Jesus for our eyes

(*MOVEMENT: Raise arms slowly up into a "V" position, with head slightly raised.*)

PRAYER: That see all the beauty of the world you made for us.

(*MOVEMENT: Bring arms down to your sides and swing them up, crossing them over in front of your body and back to the "V" position.*)

PRAYER: Please never let us be afraid to ask you to help us when we are hurt

(*MOVEMENT: Kneel on one knee and bend over a little, extending arms slightly forward.*)

PRAYER: Andlet us always believe that you can heal us.

(*MOVEMENT: Stand and raise arms back to "V" position.*)

How do you feel now that Jesus has healed us? Let us say thanks to Him for all He has done.

DANCE: "This is the Day." (*This dance is done in a circle with any number of children.*

Holding hands, the children take eight slip steps to the right.

Letting go of hands, they then take four walking steps into the centre of the circle and clap twice. Take four steps back and clap again.

Take right arm across body and raise overhead. Repeat with the left arm. Repeat with both arms at the same time. Repeat the last movement with both arms one more time.

Skip around in one circle turning to the right for eight counts. Take both arms up into the "V" position.

Standing in place, clap twice to the right side and then to the left. Repeat three times.)

The Uncreation

"The Uncreation" is based on a poem written by an unknown Jesuit priest.

This drama/mime requires a narrator and two chorus groups who have choreographed actions to perform.

CHORUS:

Group 1: Tick tock tick tock.
Group 2: Time running out.
Group 1: Tick tock tick tock.
Group 2: Time running short.

NARRATOR: In the beginning of the end, people said, "Let there be darkness." So the people built.

CHORUS:

Group 1: Cut down the trees.
Group 2: Dig up the soil.
Group 1: Pollute the streams.
Group 2: Scar the earth.
Group 1: Build up.

Group 2: Tear down.
Group 1: Tear down.
Group 2: Build up.
Group 1: Sky scrapers.
Group 2: Smoke stacks.
Group 1: Oil wells.
Group 2: Wood chips.
Group 1: Build up.
Group 2: Tear down. Tear down. Tear down.

NARRATOR: And the people called the darkness "progress."
And behold, it was grim.

The people said, "Let us gather to ourselves as much as we can of what is left of the fish of the sea, the birds of the air, and the products of the earth."

CHORUS:

Group 1: Buy.
Group 2: Buy.
Group 1: Buy up the food.
Group 2: Buy up the oil.
Group 1: More.
Group 2: More.
Group 1: Keep all the food.
Group 2: Keep all the drink.
Group 1: More.
Group 2: More.
Group 1: The economy.
Group 2: The market place.
Group 1: We must keep
Group 2: The market in place.
Group 1: The strong will survive.
Group 2: The rich will thrive.

1 Voice: And the weak will die.

NARRATOR: And the people called the gathering "wealth," and only those with "wealth" were allowed to eat, and most of the world began to starve, and behold, it was very grim.

The governments of the people told them that there was danger from other people, other governments. They needed to build weapons.

CHORUS:

Group 1: Faster, faster.
Group 2: More, more.
Group 1: We must build faster.
Group 2: We must build more.
Group 1: Enough to be strong.
Group 2: The strong will survive.
Group 1: They have more.
Group 2: We must build faster.
Group 1: We will be strong.
Group 2: And so will we.
Group 1: Faster, faster.
Group 2: More, more.
Group 1: Enough to be strong.
Group 2: Enough to destroy.
Group 1: To destroy the earth.
Group 2: Once, twice.
Group 1: Three times or more.
Group 2: We must not stop.
Group 1: We must have more.

NARRATOR: And the people called the weapon "defence." There is enough defence today to destroy the world *twenty-three times over*! And indeed it was very grim.

CHORUS:

Group 1: Tick tock tick tock.
Group 2: Time running out.
Group 1: Tick tock tick tock.
Group 2: Time running short.

NARRATOR: This story is continuing today; the ending depends on us.

Billy Tea
and Damper

In the corner country out the back of New South Wales
are a group of weathered drovers who have many
   wondrous tales.
The stories they remember to remind them of the years,
the droughts, the flood and struggle, the laughter and
   the tears.

But there's one old drover's story that stands out above
   the rest,
and of all the tales they told me it's the one I like the best.
It's about a simple drover who came off the plains one
   day
with a herd of tatty, ragged sheep, and for awhile he
   stayed.

Now this cove[1] looked nothing special, no looks to draw
   your eyes,
just a scruffy, skinny bloke with a corked hat to shoo the
   flies.
But when this man began to speak, people stopped and
   stared,

for with every word that left his mouth people saw how
    much he cared.

When you came up close to him and looked deeply in
    his face,
you could see this man had suffered by the lines the years
    had traced.
Although his life was etched in pain, he spoke only of the
    joy,
and the stories that he told them made them feel like girls
    and boys.

People came from miles around to listen to his words:
the townies left their jobs; the stockmen left their herds.
And on a barren, dusty hill about a mile from town,
the drover spoke to all of them as they pressed tightly
    round.

"Life ain't just for workin', though you gotta pay ya debts,
but what's the good of workin' if ulcers all ya gets?
No, what's the point of makin' money if you forget to
    care?
You've gotta love ya neighbour, you've gotta learn to
    share."

"Take the eucalyptus: fire opens up it's seed.
Many of the plants must die to keep alive the breed.
So this noble tree gives up all it has to give.
Like so many things in life, ya gotta die a bit to live."

While the drover talked to the people gathered round,
there was another meeting taking place back in the town.
The cockies[2] and the bosses had gathered there that day,

the subject of their conference: how to drive this bloke
away.

"Mark my words," one cockie said, "this is just the start.
Let one bloke like this in and the place will fall apart.
He talks of loving others, how we should care for all.
Next he'll bring in unions, then watch your profits fall."

They called the local trooper and told him what to do.
"We've thought through our decisions and now it's up
to you.
Tonight they'll all be eating in a pub this side of town.
You go and tell the drover we don't want his kind
around."

The trooper saw the bloke that night and made his position clear.
He said, "This is a workin' town; we don't need no
bludgers[3] here.
Now don't you get me wrong; I'm not lookin' for a fight,
but grab yer scabby sheep and go; I want you out
tonight."

The drover's friends were really mad, one went to thump
the cop.
But before his hand could knock him down, the drover
cried out, "Stop!"
"Don't raise your fists against him; this man's your
brother too.
Anyone can love a friend; I'm asking more of you."

The drover gathered up his sheep and bid his friends
goodbye.
All the people saw him off and not one eye was dry.

As the sun came up that morning, the drover walked
   away,
and no one in that district has seen him to this day.

In the town there was a feeling that no one tried to hide,
it was like a kind of mourning, as if a friend had died.
And all the people knew they'd lost someone really great:
a storyteller, a poet, a teacher, and a mate.
But the town was not the same as it had always been.
It was as if the simple drover still lingered there unseen.
You could tell there was a difference in the people living
   there.
People smiled and talked; joy drifted in the air.

Perhaps there is a reason why the town still has this feel,
for before the drover left them, he shared in one last meal.
They still eat this meal together to remind them of their
   friend:
billy tea and damper[4]; and they say he'll come again.

NOTES

1. Cove: person or fellow.

2. Cockies: property owners.

3. Bludger: one who lives off the earnings of another; a lazy person.

4. Billy tea and damper: a "billy" is a tin container with a handle, used to boil water over a campfire. "Billy tea" is simply tea made in the billy.

"Damper" is bread. It was made only from flour and water and perhaps a pinch of salt, and cooked in the ashes of the fire.

Stations of
the Cross

READER 1: Jesus is condemned to death.

READER 2: Good evening, here is the news. In Washington today, the President again urged Congress to approve $100 million in aid for the Contra rebels in El Salvador. He said that opponents of the aid were only assisting the interests of the socialist government in that country.

On the local scene, more cutbacks are expected in welfare payments as the government struggles to contain its deficit.

In Paris today, the President reinforced his government's determination to continue testing nuclear weapons on Muroa Atoll. He said that as a nuclear power, France had a right to test its weapons and that the protests of other nations in the South Pacific were futile.

READER 1: Jesus accepts his cross.

READER 2: In South Africa today, jailed political activist Nelson Mandela refused to accept government conditions attached to his release. Mr. Mandela said that he would remain in prison until he was granted an unconditional release. A spokesperson for the President said that there was little likelihood of Mr. Mandela being released unless he acceded to the government's demands.

READER 1: Jesus falls for the first time.

READER 2: Beirut, Thursday: A Palestinian woman killed herself and her four children today in a Beirut refugee camp where a fifteen-week siege by the Shi'ite Muslim militiamen has led some residents to eat rats, Palestinian sources said.

The sources said the woman set fire to herself and her children in Bourj al-Baranjnh camp because they preferred sudden death to starvation.

READER 1: Jesus meets his mother.

READER 2: The mother of a two year old with "cancer in every bone from head to toe" is leading a band of dedicated parents to raise money for cancer research. Martha Davidson is involved with the Hills District Leukemia and Cancer Support Group. With similar groups throughout the state, it is desperately trying to raise $40,000 to employ a full-time research doctor at the Oncology Unit at Camperdown Children's Hospital.

READER 1: Simon helps Jesus carry his cross.

READER 2: The Reverend Ted Knoffs opened another Life Education Centre in Sydney's western suburbs today. The centres are designed to assist young people in dealing with the pressures of growing up.

READER 1: Veronica wipes the face of Jesus.

READER 2: A dramatic dash by a team of doctors to Townsville has provided new hope for a Sydney boy dying from a liver disease. Police said that the 20-year-old man who donated the liver and kidneys had been involved in a traffic accident in the Townsville area last week.

READER 1: Jesus falls for the second time.

READER 2: South Africa's Minister of Law and Order has disclosed that 281 children under sixteen are still in detention under emergency regulations. In a statement issued in Cape Town, the Minister said three of the detainees were under twelve years old.

READER 1: Jesus speaks to the women and children.

READER 2: Archbishop Desmond Tutu arrived in Sydney this afternoon. At a press conference he underlined the fact that sanctions against South Africa were the only way of putting pressure on the white minority government.

READER 1: Jesus falls for the third time.

READER 2: Three mentally-retarded aborigines were being held in grossly inhuman conditions in Alice Springs jail, the senate heard yesterday. A Democrat senator said the men were locked in tiny cells for twenty hours a day.

READER 1: Jesus is stripped of his garments.

READER 2: Hospital fees are expected to soar in New South Wales under a radical new charging system revealed yesterday. Some charges may rise by as much as fifty per cent. The big losers under the state's new patient classification system will be those people–numbering almost a million–who have only basic health insurance cover. A spokesman of the NSW Private Hospitals Association conceded that while the new charges would be a disaster for patients in the basic table, those in the top table of benefits would be adequately covered.

READER 1: Jesus is crucified.

READER 2: A leader of Christian Action claimed today that the AIDS epidemic was God's retribution against homosexuals for what he described as "their sinful and degraded lifestyle."

READER 1: Jesus dies on the cross.

READER 2: Two hostages being held by Shi'ite Muslims in Beirut were executed today. Their bodies were dumped at the entrance of one of the local newspapers in the early hours of the morning. Israel responded immediately by bombing a section of the city under Shi'ite control. The last report estimated the death toll from the raid at fifteen, with many others missing or trapped in the rubble.

READER 1: Jesus is taken down from the cross.

READER 2: Six people died today in an apartment fire in Chicago. One of the victims, a black woman named Mrs. Johnetta Hodges, had escaped the blaze but returned to the apartment building twice to rescue her mother, son, and nephew before dying in the street.

READER 1: Jesus is laid in the tomb.

READER 2: There were emotional scenes in the small western New South Wales town of Wilcannia today at the funeral for an aboriginal youth. The boy died in police custody and leaders of the aboriginal community are demanding an inquest into his death. The local police sergeant described the present feeling between blacks and whites in the community as "extremely tense."

Sower and the Seed (3)

The following mime was developed for one mime/clown. You will need a bag large enough to climb into, as well as a number of props. The props will vary according to the needs of the individual, so I will not list them here. The script for the mime is in the form of notes to the performer. It is intended to be merely an outline, so you will need to fill in some of the details yourself. Use your imagination. Don't just take the idea as it is; play with it and see what suits you best.

Mimist enters stage area carrying large bag over shoulder, then sees audience. Mimist rolls up sleeve and reaches deep into bag and pulls out a sign that says THE SOWER AND THE SEED.

Mimist opens mouth of bag and looks in, then looks up at audience and smiles. S/he reaches deep into bag and rummages around. Mimist withdraws hand from bag, holds up thumb and forefinger pinched together. Mimist looks closely at seed and smiles.

Mimist puts seed carefully into top pocket and pats pocket. Then s/he rummages in bag again and produces a dustpan and brush.

After careful inspection of possible sites on stage, mimist cleans a small area. Then mimist puts dustpan and brush aside and takes seed proudly from pocket and places it on spot.

Mimist waits, anxiously staring at ground. Nothing happens. Mimist looks up at audience a little puzzled, then back at ground. Still nothing happens. Mimist looks bored, begins to yawn, and starts to nod off.

Suddenly, something begins to happen. Mimist looks excitedly at ground and points. Something is happening. But just as everything looks rosy, something else happens. Mimist looks up and begins to swat at air—birds. Mimist runs to bag, produces a baseball bat, and starts swiping at imaginary birds. After a few moments of mimist beating at air, birds begin to leave. Clown looks up at sky and shakes fist. Oops—mimist wipes eye. Yuck. Looks down at ground—oh no—the seed is gone. Mimist looks deflated.

Undeterred, mimist returns to bag. Mimist takes a long look into bag, then looks at audience—nothing. Mimist puts head and shoulders into bag and begins to rummage around. Finally mimist emerges from bag with thumb and forefinger pressed together.

Mimist selects another spot and plants seed. Waits. Mimist looks up at sky—it's hot. Mimist wipes sweat from brow; shoulders slump; head droops. Mimist goes to bag and produces a bottle of sunscreen and a sunhat. Mimist continues to watch seed. Look, something is happening. Seed begins to grow. Mimist encourages seed to grow. Mimist shows with body that seed grows up a little way but then wilts. Mimist is shattered. Tries to give the seed mouth to mouth or fan it with hat. No good; seed is gone. Mimist drops hat over spot and blesses it.

Mimist returns to bag. It is much harder to find a seed this time. Mimist disappears into bag, except for feet, and rummages around furiously. Finally, mime reappears with a seed.

Mimist selects spot and plants new seed. After a moment, seed begins to grow and mimist is overjoyed. Then mimist's own arm begins to grow up beside him/her. Mimist looks up at arm, shocked; hand takes on a menacing-looking claw shape, and mimist looks at audience, worried. Other arm begins to grow up as well and takes on a similar sinister position. Mimist looks really worried. Suddenly hands attack, grabbing mimist by throat, strangling him/her. Mimist crumples to ground. After a moment, mimist takes out a white handkerchief and from a prone position on ground waves the handkerchief in air.

Mimist picks self up off ground and dusts off. Deflated, s/he looks at spots on ground where seeds have died. Slowly mimist returns to bag. This time it is almost impossible to find seed. Mimist disappears into bag. Props begin flying out mouth of bag. Finally mimist emerges from bag with seed. S/he holds up one finger on other hand to indicate that this is last seed.

Mimist plants seed and waits. After a moment, seed begins to grow. Mimist looks suspiciously at it. He looks up in the air— no sun, no birds. Mimist takes a cautious look at hands and quickly places them behind back. The plant continues to grow. Mimist steps back and walks around plant. It's very big. Mimist picks some fruit from tree, shines it, and takes a bite. Mimist goes over to bag takes out a sign that says THE END.

Readers' Theatre

The idea of readers' theatre is not a new one. Many companies throughout the world (especially in the U.S.A) use this technique for presenting plays. The technique has been referred to as "theatre of the mind" as it demands that the audience use its imagination. In a play, characters are well-defined with costumes, and lighting and scenery add to the overall picture. In readers' theatre the "trimmings" are kept down to a few basic essentials, so the audience has to supply the rest. Listeners to readers' theatre must see more than just the actors. They must envision the characters, the set, and the action.

The reader can help the audience by wearing a hat, which may suggest the role s/he is playing (e.g., a police officer), or s/he may use a cane and wear spectacles, which would perhaps suggest age. An actor on stage could change position on the stage to suggest taking on a new character. What we call "symbolic cues" can be used to also help stimulate the listeners' senses (e.g., actors may read the lines from a ladder if they are playing Goliath or from a wheel chair if they are playing a paralytic).

What Are the Characteristics of Readers' Theatre?

Let's have a look at what characteristics are common in readers' theatre.

(a) The actors read from their scripts. I particularly like readers' theatre because it means that I don't have to worry about learning lines, although it is essential for actors to know their lines thoroughly so as not to bury their heads in their script.

The scripts are usually uniform in size and design, although a script can be used to suggest a character (e.g., with Goliath a large script can be used, or a script shaped like an apple can suggest Eve.

(b) Biblical material is suitable for readers' theatre. You are only limited by your imagination. Poetry, short stories, or songs can also be used. Perhaps a night of readers' theatre would present various stories, poetry, and scripture revolving around a theme such as forgiveness.

(c) Changes in characters can be shown by changing voice, stance, a costume item, a level. The characters represented in the readers' theatre are not meant to be complete; therefore one can change from one character to another with the simplest of ease.

(d) While the reading is taking place, the reader does not look at the other characters, not even when the characters are engaged in dialogue with each other. The readers focus on a fixed point, which is usually somewhere in the audience, to suggest this exchange of dialogue.

The following diagram shows five readers (A,B,C,D,E). When A is in dialogue with B, the common point of focus is shown by X. When B is is dialogue with C, the common point of focus is shown by X. When A is in dialogue with C, the common point of focus is shown by Y. The common point of focus is, therefore, somewhere between the two actors engaged in dialogue.

Reader A   Reader B   Reader C   Reader D   Reader E

X   Y   X

(e) Any action that takes place within a script is done symbolically (e.g., sleep may be suggested with the actor's head lowered, with chin resting on his/her chest; the man walking from Jericho to Jerusalem may be presented as walking on the spot.

(f) Costumes are kept to a minimum. I like to see all the actors in some basic costume, perhaps black shirt and black trousers. Then some simple props can be used to help create the character, *but* remember not to overdue this. Makeup is kept to a minimum.

(g) The only settings that are used are stools for each of the actors and the few simple props to help set the scene (e.g., the ladder for Goliath).

(h) Lighting, music, and sound effects can also be used to help create the desired atmosphere.

From Bible to Performance

The question now is what material to perform as readers' theatre.

Choose stories that have dramatic interest (i.e., stories with characters, interaction, conflict—all the elements of good drama.

Choose stories that are rich in language and imagery.

Do not be discouraged if you do not have enough readers to play all the parts. In readers' theatre it is acceptable for one person to read several parts.

When adapting a bible story for readers' theatre, be sure that the final performance script is coherent.

What Does Readers' Theatre Offer?

As I mentioned before, I particularly enjoy readers' theatre because I need not memorize pages and pages of a script. This does not mean, however, that I need not be totally familiar with the script. Holding the script is totally acceptable.

Readers' theatre stimulates the imagination of the viewer.

It is an inexpensive way of producing drama, as very little is needed in the way of props and scenery.

You do not have to search for appropriate dramas to interpret if you adapt biblical stories.

The potential of readers' theatre as a means of presenting the Word is unlimited.

Play with the concept of readers' theatre, enjoy it, and, above all, use it.

James, John, Zebedee, and Norma

Whatever happened to Zebedee after James and John went off with Jesus? Here is one possible answer. Use your imagination to think of possible endings to other open-ended stories. They can be used to reinforce the original bible story.

NORMA: Ohh, just wait till I get my hands on those men. I'll teach them to come home late. It won't be my fault if their dinner is burned to a crisp. They don't care about me. Oh no, here I am slaving away all day in the house, washing, cleaning, working my fingers to the bone and for what—what thanks do I get? Nothing—I could die for all they care. Hang on; that sounds like them now. Zebedee, is that you? Get in here and bring those two good-for-nothing boys of yours with you. Zebedee! ZEBEDEE!!

ZEBEDEE: Ah, yes, Sugarplum? Did I hear you bellow?

NORMA: Yes you did. Where've you been? I don't expect much, you know, just a little consideration from time to time. If you're going to be late you could call, just take a moment or two of your precious time to let your poor overworked wife know where you are, but I suppose that that would be asking too much. How are you anyway? Have a good day fishing while I was breaking my back cleaning up after you? Get a nice tan did you? Don't blame me if your dinner is burned.

ZEBEDEE: But honeybunch, you were preparing salad for dinner.

NORMA: I know, but when you were late I put it into the oven. Here, I hope the tomato's not too dry for you.

ZEBEDEE: Eh, thank you, sweetness. I don't feel all that hungry actually.

NORMA: Typical. I practically kill myself getting it ready and now you don't want it. Don't worry about the wasted effort. I'll just offer it up as another one of the crosses I have to bear. Speaking of crosses, where are James and John, off sunbaking are they or making another mess for me to clean up, I suppose?

ZEBEDEE: Well, er, I was meaning to speak to you about that, dearest. The boys won't be home for dinner at all tonight.

NORMA: Oh great, just terrific, that's three dinners wasted. Don't worry about me; I'm just the hired help. And just where are they, if I may ask?

ZEBEDEE: Well that's hard to say exactly, dear.

NORMA: What do you mean, "hard to say exactly"? They were with you, weren't they? You did go fishing together, didn't you?

ZEBEDEE: Yes, yes we did, butterfly, but they sort of...left after awhile.

NORMA: Surely they told you where they were going?

ZEBEDEE: No, they didn't, but I wouldn't blame them, dewdrop. I don't think they knew exactly where they were going themselves.

NORMA: Didn't know! You mean you just let my two babies wander off into the desert alone?

ZEBEDEE: Well, that's just what I'm getting at, sweetness, they weren't alone; they went off with this messiah chappie.

NORMA: With who?

ZEBEDEE: This young, long-haired fellow came by and before I knew what was happening, James and John had trotted off after him. Left me to pull in the nets by myself; I nearly ruptured myself in the process. I must say I was dashed annoyed at the time.

NORMA: You let my children be kidnapped by a hippie!

ZEBEDEE: Well, he seemed quite a decent chap. He talked quite a bit about the Kingdom of heaven and loving one another and so on, frightfully well spoken.

NORMA: Oh dear! My boys have been lured into some kind of weird religious sect. We'll never see them again. Who knows what kind of bizarre rituals they'll be involved in, and you, their own father, didn't have the sense to stop them.

ZEBEDEE: But dearest, I tried. By the time I got the nets out of the water the boys were long gone. Anyway, what was I supposed to do? This messiah was not alone; he had two other largish fellows with him.

NORMA: You mean there was a whole gang of them? That's it then; my children have been taken by terrorists. I told you we should never have moved to the Middle East. How will we ever raise the ransom?

ZEBEDEE: Now don't get overwrought, dear. I'm sure the boys will be just fine. They followed off after this fellow of their own accord. I'm sure they'll come home when they get bored or hungry.

NORMA: That's easy for you to say, you pseudo-father. You let your kids just wander off when you're supposed to be looking after them and then you hope they'll just wander home again. That's not good enough for me. I'm going to find this hippie kidnapper and bring my babies home.

ZEBEDEE: But honeypie, we don't know where they went.

NORMA: They shouldn't be hard to find. I'll just keep an eye out for those psychedelic hippie commune vans.

Put the Lively Arts To Work In Your Ministry!

Worship Through The Seasons: *Ideas for Celebration*
by Mary Isabelle Hock
Paperbound, $7.95
106 pages, 5½"x8½"
ISBN 0-89390-104-0

Make your assembly part of the action - with help from these songs, dramatic sketches, pageants, movement scripts, and symbolic actions. Sections on Advent, Christmas, Epiphany, Lent, Easter, and Pentecost. Easy to follow. Easy to do. Involves children and adults - in any creative congregation. Special section on home celebrations.

Come Mime With Me
by Gail Kelley and Carol Hershberger
Paperbound, $9.95
90 pages, 8½"x11"
ISBN 0-89390-089-3

With insight into the performing abilities of children, the authors have developed a "can't miss" formula for presenting children's drama. They show you how to write your own dramas using a narration led by an adult and parts acted out by children. They then share scripts from 10 dramas that they have presented successfully.

Actions, Gestures, and Bodily Attitudes
by Carolyn Deitering
Paperbound, $10.95
96 pages, 8½"x11"
ISBN 0-89390-021-4

A classic work examining basic Christian ritual actions and bodily movement as prayer forms.
"Showing us the affinity of gesture and the scriptural word, Carolyn explores clearly how to place ourselves at the meeting place of body, prayer, and dance."
— Carla Desola

How The Word Became Flesh, by Michael Moynahan, SJ
Paperbound, $10.95
135 pages, 6"x9"
ISBN 0-89390-029-X

Bring scripture lessons to life with this collection of simple-to-use story dramas that embody the deepest gospel messages. Complete staging instructions make these easy-to-use in church with adults or in school with young adults!

Order these books from your local bookstore, or send this form along with your payment to:

Resource Publications, Inc.
160 E. Virginia St., Suite 290
San Jose, CA 95112-5848

Qty.	Title	Amt.
___	_____	____
___	_____	____
___	_____	____
___	_____	____

Postage and handling
$1.50 for orders under $10.00
$2.00 for orders of $10.00-$25.00
9% of order for orders over $25.00
CA residents add 6% sales tax. _____

WD   Total _____

___My check or money order is enclosed.
___Charge my credit card (minimum order, $25.00).
___VISA ___MC
Exp. date _____
Card No. _____
Signature _____
Name _____
Address _____
City/St./Zip _____
Phone (_____) _____